Dog Training

for

Managers

Dog Training
for
Managers

THE ELEMENTS OF LEADING INTELLIGENT CREATURES WELL

Douglas C. Morgan

authorHOUSE®

AuthorHouse™
1663 Liberty Drive
Bloomington, IN 47403
www.authorhouse.com
Phone: 1 (800) 839-8640

Published by AuthorHouse 07/09/2015

ISBN: 978-1-5049-1909-8 (sc)
ISBN: 978-1-5049-1908-1 (e)

Library of Congress Control Number: 2015910092

Print information available on the last page.

This book is printed on acid-free paper.

With gratitude to those who have shown me good leadership and in honor of those who have allowed me to lead them, be they human or canine

I am still learning.

Douglas C. Morgan

"When the effective leader is finished with his work,
the people will say it happened naturally."

— Lao Tse

Contents

Preface

Whether you are a seasoned veteran or new to your role, *Dog Training for Managers* will teach you how to bring out the very best in those who depend upon you for care and direction.

As its title purports, this book will show experienced managers how to apply their leadership skills to the challenges of training dogs. Our method will be to observe philosophies and techniques that good managers use for purposeful human leadership and apply these to the relatively uncomplicated challenge presented by a dog's training needs. As you readily achieve the rewards of success in this more straightforward environment, you will reinforce your leadership skills for many purposes. The best practices for the caring leadership of intelligent creatures are broadly applicable.

Of course, the real mission of this book is not about training your dog; it is about educating you. Unless your dog is exceptional beyond precedent, only you can learn directly what this book seeks to teach. While it is helpful for both trainer and trainee to understand the training process fully, sharing such an understanding is difficult when your student lacks your intelligence. As you know from your experience as a manager, even if your subordinate is as intelligent as you, you cannot expect him to share your experience, perception, or adaptability. A key challenge in your leadership role is to understand needs and motivations from both perspectives well enough that you and your followers can mutually benefit from your leadership.

Many of the requirements for leading well, be it in managing humans or training dogs, are universal. Both activities require having clear goals. Both demand an unrelenting focus on effective communication. Both entail ongoing exchanges and acknowledgments. Both work best in an environment of mutual understanding and respect.

While, as the leader, you may seek to modify the behavior of your follower, truly effective leadership requires that you first modify your own behavior in response to the behavior of your follower. The key is to teach him through your responses that if he does what you want him to do, you will do what he wants you to do. Effective leadership is good for both parties.

I have developed my perspective through years of experiences as a dog owner, a caregiver, a father, a manager, a teacher, a student, a subordinate, a son, a dependent, and always, as a dog, in virtually every sense of the word. Lest you mistake this dissertation by its title to debase the hallowed relationship between a manager and his subordinate or to confuse a fellow human with a canine possession, permit me to assert emphatically that I am sensitive to the differences on many levels. I am simply celebrating the enlightenment that one can obtain through abstraction and analysis of the familiar characteristics of one species when working with another. As I use human management analogies to illustrate applications to canine training, should I cause concern that I have failed to honor fundamental differences separating the species, please give it a little time, and I believe you will find that I eventually do address the distinctions adequately and respectfully.

While my rudimentary intention in writing this book has been to illustrate how to apply well-proven approaches used for leading people to the arguably simpler challenge of training dogs, if you can extract what works when training dogs and apply it *appropriately* to managing people, then I would suggest that to be a real added benefit of your study. Moreover, if you enjoy what you read or learn, then that is the best for which I could possibly hope.

A Couple of Dog Stories

Over the years, I have learned much from dogs. When I was a teenager, our family dog was an Irish wolfhound named Erin. She was never trained to do anything beyond sit, shake, and come (and barely that). When she responded to any commands, it was according to her own agenda. Everyone who knew Erin showered her with love and lavish affection; she was never the target of any serious human aggression. The only time anyone ever yelled at her was to get her out of the street, as she showed no appreciation for the dangers of automobiles, which she considered her approximate equal in size.

Erin was a huge but gentle dog who could recognize when she was striking terror into others intimidated by her size. Whenever people showed any signs of fear, she would back off and assume a submissive position, so we never worried about her interactions with people. Admittedly, those experiencing the terror did not always recognize her gentle submission. Were we to have been more responsible owners, we would have worried more about their feelings, although no real harm ever came from our negligence.

Erin was as friendly as a dog could possibly be to man and beast. She would swim after the swans in the local park pond but retreat quickly when they became aggressive in telling her they did not want to play. Once, when attacked by a German shepherd mirroring his master's nasty personality, she swatted the dog down using only her paws (and not her jaws, with which she could have permanently dispatched him). I remember pleading with the other man to get his dog back on leash, and to this day I am certain this poor excuse for an owner was disappointed he did not get more of a spectacle from the encounter. I remember this incident with anger and dismay. I am disgusted whenever I observe anything like it because this is truly a human and not a canine problem.

As happy and socially well-adjusted as Erin was, I still think we shortchanged her safety and well-being by failing to provide her with formal training. Erin was as much as we could have wanted in a pet, but we were not as much as we should have been as her caretakers, for her sake and the sakes of others. While wolfhounds may not be the intellectual laureates of the canine world, I do know they can learn. I recall how happy Erin looked when being praised for shaking hands properly. We probably missed many opportunities for such happy interaction. We were lucky this gentle giant never ran into a car or provoked a heart attack while merrily engaging people who were unaware of her gentleness.

Indeed, no big problems ever developed from our benign neglect of Erin's formal training; her good nature and our good luck prevailed to the end. In a way, however, I suppose she was trained. Everyone always treated her kindly. She perceived no threats from anyone or anything, and she reflected that in her gentle behavior toward others.

****

A few years later, while I was away at college, I lived with two people in a farmhouse on about five acres of open land north of the university. Both roommates were dog lovers; each had two dogs that played outside all day but came inside when we were home.

One day, a stray dog came to visit. He just wandered up and started to hang out with the rest of the pack. He appeared to be some indiscriminate blend of Airedale and German shepherd well into his middle years. He was the oldest, biggest, and immediately most dominant of the five, yet he was friendly, both with the other dogs and with their humans. We noticed he was sleeping on the outside doorstep in the evenings, while our other dogs all slept inside. He had no tags, and we could find no evidence that any previous owner was looking for him. In an attempt to encourage him to return home, we did not feed him for several days, although he did help himself to water in the bowls we left outside for the other dogs. He was a strange but likable dog that simply would not leave.

After almost a week of waiting for our new visitor to wander on, I had him hop in my car for a trip to the local veterinarian, who confirmed that he was in good health, albeit quite malnourished. On the spot, I got him a rabies shot, a leather dog collar, a flea collar, a food bowl, and a tag engraved with the name "Stranger." Stranger and I returned home that evening just about feeding time.

As my housemates and I were typical students with unscheduled comings and goings, it was up to whoever was home to make sure the dogs were fed. Our routine was to feed all the dogs together every night a little before our human dinnertime. Each dog had its own food bowl; they shared a large water tub. Picking up the food bowls and placing them on the kitchen counter to be filled signaled the approach of dinner. The sound of the bowls would trigger a stampede of the dogs to the kitchen from throughout the house. For the sake of order, all were trained to sit in a corner of the kitchen while the bowls were filled and placed on the floor. Upon the issuance of an "Okay!" all would run to their individual bowls and begin eating, rarely with any conflicts. Each dog had a personal style and speed of eating, but the routine was common. As each dog finished eating, it would usually get a drink of water and wander off to another part of the house; each had a favorite place. All of the dogs had the dining routine down pat, and it worked well.

I was the only person home that evening when I came back with Stranger, the new pet. Upon arriving, I opened the back door as usual, and the other four dogs merrily romped in after me, in anticipation of dinner. Stranger eagerly came in with the others as he had wanted to earlier in the week, somehow aware that he was now one of the "inside" dogs.

That first evening, without giving it much thought, I decided to fill the new bowl for Stranger and assumed that since the other four dogs knew their bowls, Stranger would figure out which was his. I was successful in getting him to sit in the corner with the others; he had obviously had some proper upbringing at one time. However, as the first four dogs sat in patient anticipation, the sounds and smell of the food drove Stranger absolutely crazy. He wildly showed his anticipation for his first meal in days by jumping up and down on all four legs in a boisterous display of uncontrolled excitement. It took only about took two milliseconds for the other dogs to break with the routine and join in the pandemonium.

Immediately, I stopped the food preparation and waited for the dogs to calm down and return to their proper positions. I even got Stranger to sit quietly with the others until I returned to the preparation activities, when again all hell broke loose. After a few more attempts, I accepted the futility of the situation and gently but forcefully threw Stranger out the back door, very much against his will. While he sat outside barking at the door, the rest dined according to the accepted routine. After all had eaten and run off to their usual after-dinner locations, I let Stranger back in, brought him to the kitchen, and one-on-one put him through the standard routine of sitting in the corner until given the okay. I had to pick his bowl back up several times before he got it, but get it he did. He spent that night on the floor of my bedroom, clearly happy for the care from his new human friend and benefactor.

The next evening, one of my housemates prepared the food while I focused on keeping Stranger sitting in line with the others. It did take quite a few attempts. His first choice was, unfortunately, the bowl of the most dominant dog of the original four. Quick anticipation allowed me to restrain Stranger and force him to sit back in the waiting area while my housemate moved his bowl farther from the other bowls. Upon my housemate giving the okay, I released Stranger, and he ran to his bowl. Dinner proceeded according to expectations. Within a few days, all five dogs were following the routine faithfully and harmoniously.

A few key things I learned from this experience have stayed with me over the years:

- You definitely can teach an old dog new tricks.

- If you want to achieve an expected behavior, you must insist upon it (and, ideally, from the very beginning).

- If your first approach does not work, it is up to you to change your approach to meet the training needs of your dog.

- Once your dog realizes that a particular behavior is expected and will be rewarded, he will come to demonstrate the behavior reliably unless seriously distracted, as were the original four dogs at dinner on Stranger's first day.

I am convinced that much like people, dogs actually enjoy routine and predictability of results. Frankly, I enjoy getting the behavior I seek, conformance with my need for order, if not control, as well as the opportunity to reward my dog for having pleased me. I think most people do. It is not unlike the happy feeling that a good manager gets when he rewards his people for performing well on the goals he has set with them.

Introduction

Throughout my life, as I have enjoyed meeting and getting to know a variety of creatures representing numerous species, I have taken particular delight recognizing common behavioral characteristics shared by humans and their canine pets. As intelligent social animals seeking the best for ourselves, we share many common motivations and methods for achieving what we need and want from others. I believe that good leadership, whether manifested through managing or training, relies on essentially the same laws of social interaction regardless of the species of the follower. As this premise is core to the motivation for my book, I would like to begin by sharing some experiences that have led me to propose it.

I grew up in a midwestern city where most of my neighbors had dogs. In those days, dogs were often allowed to run free and mingle unrestrained with other inhabitants of the neighborhood. While the human adults were usually off in some other place like at work or inside the house, our space was the outdoors. Our society consisted of the children and the other socially interacting creatures of the neighborhood, mostly dogs.

We had all kinds of children and all kinds of dogs. Some were smart, some were friendly, some were possessive, and some were clearly not brought up right. Some were outgoing and loved playing with others, some were a little shy, and some were absolutely no fun at all. While most were quiet and docile, a few were noisy and aggressive. The families these children and dogs came from were just as varied, although within each family were many similarities.

Even when I visited other neighborhoods, one thing always struck me: If I knew the children or the families, I could usually match the people with their pets because of the way they acted. It had little to do with the human or canine bloodlines and more to do with the patterns of social interaction within their families. For the most part, friendly people had friendly dogs, and mean people had mean dogs. Families with fathers who had gentle ways and slow tempers and with mothers who called firmly but sweetly when it was time to come in from play not only had children who were more fun, they had dogs that were friendlier and more responsive. Families with unpleasant fathers and mothers who screeched angrily not only had children who did not get along as well with others, they had dogs that were more aggressive and less well behaved.

As I experienced more of the world, I often had my early observations about relationships among families and their pets confirmed, albeit not always in a canine context. The schools I attended where the faculty tended to be authoritarian and to invoke harsh discipline for minor infractions usually had students who showed aggressive behavior toward others in the school, as well as outsiders. Schools lacking involved faculty and families were usually not effective in their educational missions, because the students also tended to be less engaged or goal-oriented. Schools in which the leadership was clear on mission, that was balanced and disciplined in approach, and that engaged students in purposeful rapport nearly always produced better-behaved and better-educated graduates who showed respect for each other and the world around them.

Similarly, I have found that well-managed organizations with people-oriented visionary leaders who communicate a sense of organizational purpose have happier and more productive work associates, whereas supervisors who drive their staff like a prison chain gang justly wind up with employees who play that role true to script.

The effects of leaders on the behaviors of those they lead are unmistakable, whether they are parents, school administrators, or managers. Nowhere is this demonstrated more dramatically than in the effect that an owner has on the behavior of a dog.

One might contend that this matching-behavior effect in dogs follows from the often-observed correlation of an owner's personality with the breed of dog he chooses. Humans usually try to acquire things that complement the image they wish to project. Similar affiliations are true for the homes, cars, and vacations that people choose. However, the personality of a dog is not necessarily what the owner chooses it to be. Rather, it is what the owner makes it to be. While the chosen breed may reflect a desired image, the personality of a dog reflects the reality of its caretaker's interaction with it.

One of the most aggressive and unfriendly dogs that I have ever known belonged to a man who ordinarily appeared pleasant enough. This puzzled me until one day, I observed his façade collapse when a waiter at a restaurant disappointed him in some minor way. Rather than address the waiter's oversight in a nonoffensive, constructive way, his disappointment led to a tirade of verbal abuse. I dread to imagine what his pet must have suffered in private for its minor transgressions.

In contrast, one of the best-natured dogs I have ever known was close in breed to the dog I just described. This dog belonged to a manager who was highly regarded as a boss—one who expected a lot but also recognized his people's efforts and accomplishments enthusiastically. Watching him with his dog was enlightening. He directed almost all of the tricks he wanted his dog to perform using simple hand gestures and encouraging sounds. I never heard him raise his voice to his dog, even when reprimanding an unsatisfactory performance. This man's dog was friendly and engaging with everyone without being bothersome, quite unlike the other dog, which growled menacingly and bared its fangs whenever anyone looked at him.

Comfortable and gentle treatment elicits the same from those trained in that manner. Erratic treatment by one responsible for care is, at a minimum, disconcerting to one who is dependent, because it undermines a sense of security. How could anyone possibly expect to achieve calm and composed behavior without mirroring that through example?

I have observed the many similarities between respected leaders of people and owners of happy, well-behaved dogs. The most prominent shared traits are a genuine concern for the well-being of their followers and an acceptance of the responsibility to provide leadership. Good managers and good dog owners always keep their purpose for leading in mind and build their followers' commitment to that purpose by rewarding compliance with their direction. Good leaders distinguish their followers' necessities from their desirables and provide systems of rewards that conditionally provide what is wanted without threatening what is needed. The best managers and trainers adapt discerningly to the individuals they lead.

I have also observed that poor managers and bad owners share some common negative traits. The worst of these demonstrate flagrant disrespect for others and impose demands without purpose or support. Selfish, erratic, and unfocused directive behavior causes frustration. Any loss of self-control by a manager or trainer, particularly when it results in aggression toward those being led, is a very serious problem. However, simply failing to recognize and reward good behavior can diminish leadership effectiveness.

A less heinous but nonetheless debilitating flaw shared by many poor managers and trainers is the lack of an internal vision. Those unclear on what it is they want to accomplish are unlikely to obtain satisfying results from those they presume to lead.

In any position of leadership authority, the leader has the prerogative—indeed, the responsibility—to define and obtain desired behaviors. By defining what he wants in a thoughtful process before attempting to lead, the good leader establishes an opportunity for success. By learning effective and humane leadership techniques, a leader improves his chances for success along with the chances of success for those led.

Throughout training, strive to improve the happiness and well-being of your student while achieving behaviors that are consistent with your expectations. Leading in any other way is unethical, disrespectful, and counterproductive to developing a good subordinate or a happy companion. Especially with your pet, your intentions should always be noble, because it is by your choice to be its owner that your pet became helplessly dependent on you for most of what it needs.

I expect that by your experience as a successful manager, you have indeed learned and demonstrated effective leadership skills that are ethical and respectful: ones that achieve the behaviors you seek while showing suitable concern for the welfare of those you lead. From your management experience, you know that an unwavering focus on your core goals is crucial for defining the results you seek. Just as important, you know that motivating your people to learn your goals and to want to help accomplish them is crucial to getting the results you seek.

In this book, as we strive to develop dog-training skills, we will focus on four principles that are fundamental to any form of effective training, regardless of the species you seek to lead:

- **Know what it is that you wish to train.**

This, of course, raises the question of why you are training in the first place. Without a clear understanding of why you are training or what you wish to train, you cannot hope to instill the desired behavior in others.

- **Have consistent systems of meaningful incentives in operation at all times.**

The next step is to understand your student's motivations, because that will define what systems will work. Incentives must actually be perceived as rewards satisfying the student's desire. Reprimands must be hit the target without unintentionally breaking the trust bond. Any effective system of incentives must provide predictable and meaningful responses specific to demonstrated behavior.

- **Observe and understand the effect of your behavior on the behavior of your student.**

Each action you take causes a reaction in your student. Through thoughtful observation of your actions and your student's reactions to them, you can obtain the insight that will empower you to understand what affects your performance as a trainer. Coupling this insight with a lot of self-discipline, you can play the right role at the right time to get the right results.

- **Be willing and able to change your actions to meet the requirements of the situation.**

It is natural and good that your students teach you as you teach them. This is an integral part of any training endeavor; effective training is a reciprocal process. As the leader, you should be the one better equipped to recognize what is happening in your interactions and the one better able to adapt. This superior ability to adapt is what allows you to stay in charge, because you respond to your students in way that motivates their acceptance of your leadership.

****

With the first of these four principles, you establish mission and purpose. Through the second, you develop the tools you need to mold your students effectively. Through the third, you acquire the wisdom to lead intelligently. However, it is the fourth principle that makes the greatest difference. The willingness and discipline to match one's behavior appropriately to each situation is a crucial leadership attribute that so many managers sadly lack. Accepting the necessity and actually mastering the ability to adapt differentiates the great teacher from the lesser one. I will strive to encourage this exceptional leadership trait through constant reminders of the need to adapt your behavior to your purpose and the situation.

****

Looking ahead, this book consists of three major parts. Part 1 develops some formal training concepts, terminology, and techniques that will serve as foundation for the remainder of our study. As you will see, especially in the abstract, the basics of good leadership are very much the same regardless of whether you are a manager of humans or a trainer of dogs. In Part 2, we address the practical applications of developing useful commands and desirable behaviors. These will be much easier once we understand the underlying theoretical material presented in Part 1. Part 3 addresses the advanced topics of adapting to different social situations, changing established rules and behaviors, and finally, that ever-challenging subject of dealing with different personalities. Enjoy your reading!

Part One

ACADEMIC FOUNDATIONS

TERMINOLOGY, THEORY, AND TECHNIQUES

Part One

SECTION ONE

Important Terminology

A Definition of Training

We start our study of "*training*" with a formal definition of the term. The Latin derivation of the word "training" suggests a form of coaxing or pulling: leading from the front. *Webster's Dictionary* defines "training" as the "act, process, or method of one who trains." With the transitive form of the verb, that is, the form referring to an action by the trainer on the trainee, one definition is "to lead or direct the growth of; to form by bending, pruning, etc." Another definition is "to form by instruction, discipline, drill, etc.; narrowly, to teach so as to be fitted, qualified, proficient, etc." A third is "to make prepared for a test, as by exercising, dieting, etc." A fourth, somewhat different meaning, is "to aim at an object; bring to bear; as, to *train* guns on the enemy."

Consider the verbs used in these definitions: "lead," "form," "teach," "make prepared," and "aim." Each specifies a deliberate action; each connotes change; each alludes to some preconceived target to be achieved by the training. The influence of the trainer on the object of his training stands out as a common thread in all these definitions.

Defining the intransitive form of the verb, *Webster's* provides "to subject oneself or to be subjected to instruction, drilling, regular exercises, dieting, etc." and "to form habits or impact proficiency by teaching, drilling, etc." Again, the implication of deliberate action reflecting a desire to achieve a specific target is evident.

In this book, we define "*training*" to mean "an action by a 'trainer' that enables or effects change in the abilities or behaviors of the 'student.'" Training will be considered as having been done when the student's knowledge or behavior is affected. The verb, as we will use it, is transitive.

We observe each act of training in three dimensions:

- good versus bad

- effective versus ineffective

- intentional versus unintentional

Training is good or bad according to the result; good training produces desirable results, while bad training produces undesirable results. The dimension of effectiveness measures the degree of influence that the training has on the knowledge or behavior of the student. In our third dimension, we observe the degree to which the training is intentional. Training can occur intentionally or haphazardly; that is, with or without an identified intentional target or even without any intention by a trainer to effect change in a student.

Our target throughout this book will be about learning how to provide *good*, *effective*, and *intentional* training consistently as appropriate to our leadership role.

Our Characters and Their Roles

Our main characters in this book are the *leaders* and their would-be *followers*. Important leadership considerations like the source of empowerment to lead, the ethical responsibilities when leading, the boundaries of what constitutes appropriate interaction, and especially, given our goals with this book, the ability to train effectively all depend upon the relationship between leader and follower. While your proper role in the leadership of your dog is quite different from the managerial role that you play with your subordinates at work, many aspects of human leadership are germane to dog training.

To evoke nuance of the highly varied roles that leaders and followers play, I employ named characters in the chapters ahead. The most common character names I have chosen to portray our leadership roles are "owner," "caretaker," "manager," and "trainer." Similarly, I refer to the object nouns of our leadership verbs, that is, our intended followers, using the terms "student," "subordinate," "dependent," and, of course, "dog."

In this chapter, we consider what is special about each character name. In later chapters, while I may appear to swap these character names somewhat freely, I do so to emphasize the specific role of the character in the situation. These character names are certainly not always interchangeable. For example, a respectful manager would never refer to his human subordinate as his dog nor would any astute human subordinate wishing to climb the corporate ladder ever claim publicly to be a dependent of his caretaker.

Our Leader Characters

Leaders are characters who influence others by directing or inspiring them to promote the leader's agenda. Effective leaders vary the way in which they play their roles, depending upon whom they are leading and the leadership objective of the situation. As the owner and presumed leader of your dog, you must take on certain aspects of each leadership character we examine here.

The Owner

The name "*Owner*" is our strongest subject noun in terms of its authority as well as responsibility. An owner's authority and his responsibility both come from the fact that he owns the object of his leadership; it is his possession.

Ownership implies rights of complete control, including, for living possessions, the power to decide about the very life of the possession. While many might question the prudence of these actions, few would deny the right of an owner to paint his rare stamp collection bright orange, set fire to his cash, or plow under his blooming flower garden. These options come as part of being an owner. However, such prerogatives make ownership relationships with other humans unquestionably inappropriate.

Obviously, the term "owner" does not describe managers with respect to the people they manage. One might even protest using the term "owner" when it comes to any other living creature (or at least one of such high echelon as a dog). While I do not intend to argue this point, I will attempt to mitigate such concern by coupling the word "owner" with the immense responsibility that comes with ownership.

Because an owner's power of control over his possession approaches absolute, so does his responsibility for it. An owner is responsible for the control and protection of his possession. An owner is responsible for maintaining his possession in such a way that he can derive the value he expects from it. If he fails at this, any loss incurred by the owner is appropriately his problem.

Any disturbance or harm to another party by his possession is the owner's legal liability. As options for control of his possession are the purview of the owner, he must ensure that his possession does not create any hazard for others. Just as an owner must face the consequences of a tree he owns falling on a neighbor's house, so must the dog owner take complete responsibility for any actions by the dog that affect others. Proper training of a dog for the safety and welfare of others is an important step toward meeting the owner's responsibility.

If a possession has any inherent rights whatsoever, the owner is responsible for ensuring that those rights are upheld and that all entitled needs are satisfied. I would argue without reservation that as intelligent creatures, dogs do have inherent rights. As a consequence of ownership, a dog owner is responsible for the feeding, health maintenance, general comfort, and happiness of his pet.

I believe most dog owners would embrace an image of being generous, nurturing, and proud owners and would shun an image of being selfish, greedy, or careless. The ideal owner is one who cares for his possession (and those affected by it) in the way that he should.

The Caretaker

To emphasize certain crucial responsibilities of a leader, I choose the noun "*Caretaker*" as another leadership character name. The caretaker's role is to ensure the protection and well-being of the object of his care. Unlike the owner, the caretaker's role has legitimacy with respect to both human and nonhuman objects, in large part because a mere caretaker is not entitled to certain prerogatives of an owner.

The authority of the caretaker to perform his role is granted by the object of his care (or by its owner). A caretaker may exert control for the good of the object, but unlike an owner, the caretaker has no right to exert control for his own pleasure (or any other selfish purpose). The caretaker has no inherent rights or authorities beyond those needed to carry out the caretaking responsibility. Rather, the caretaker is purely in a position of service.

While performing the role of a caretaker, one often establishes a dependency relationship. The greater the dependency on the caretaker, the greater the caretaker's responsibility for his charge, because the caretaker is the one who enabled that dependency. Taking on ownership of a dog establishes an almost total dependency relationship.

We have high and virtuous expectations of good caretakers. We value traits of responsibility, reliability, and trustworthiness. Good caretakers are always there to provide what is needed. Bad caretakers bring to mind selfish and neglectful traits or (even worse) those who would profit at a cost to the object of their care.

The role of the caretaker is the most narrowly defined of our leader characters. There is no compromise or ambiguity in the ideal caretaker's role; it is very one-sided. The ideal caretaker's just reward is satisfaction with the welfare of the object of his care.

The Manager

Consider our next character name, *"Manager."* While we can recognize many common attributes with the owner and the caretaker, the manager actually has a quite distinct role. Perhaps most important is the difference in how the manager is empowered to lead. Unlike the entitlement that comes with ownership, the one who submits to being managed empowers the manager's leadership role. An organization may designate a particular person as a manager, and it may designate a framework for that manager to provide direction to others in the organization. However, that manager can manage effectively only with the approval and cooperation of those managed—a fact sadly lost on poor managers and poorly managed organizations.

Unlike the caretaker, the manager's primary responsibility is to the organization in which he manages rather than to those whom he manages. The manager's role is one of an intermediary agent empowered by those he manages to focus them on the objectives set for them by the organization. While the manager does have responsibilities to those managed, to put their interests above those of the organization is a serious break from the manager's proper role. The support and care shown by a manager to those he manages must be consistent with what the organization intends.

On the other hand, this focused orientation of the manager toward serving the organization should not suggest abandoning caretaker responsibilities for those managed. Proper care is necessary to optimize performance, which is why effective good managers intentionally provide proper care to those they manage. Given the immense value of an organization's human assets, a sensible self-interest similar to that motivating an owner should naturally motivate the caretaker aspects of a manager's job. Managing valuable human assets according to the best interests of the organization does indeed afford the manager the satisfactions of an ideal caretaker as a part of the reward for doing a good job.

A manager, guided by the organization's requirements, serves the subordinates who have empowered him by leading them to achieve the organization's purpose for employing them. Performing in accordance with the organization's purpose for them is, after all, what subordinates enlist to do in exchange for the benefits they hope to derive by being in the organization. It is the bargain they engaged by joining the organization: fair compensation for good performance!

The better that subordinates are managed, the more value they contribute, and consequently, the more valuable they are to the organization. Increasing the value of his subordinates to the organization is the greatest contribution that could be expected of a manager, either by the organization he serves or by those he manages. The ideal manager's role is clear; he produces what the organization wants through those he leads, thereby benefiting both parties to his agency. Managing your dog to perform in a way that is compatible with your "organization" is also a service to both.

The Trainer

Now we turn our attention to the last of our four leader character names, the *"Trainer,"* which is the particular leadership role we are seeking to master through this study. Similar to that of a manager, a trainer's empowerment to train comes from those trained. The trainer's role is enabled by the possession of some knowledge or skill that is of perceived value to those being trained. The greater the value perceived of the trainer or of his subject matter by those he seeks to train, the easier it is to train. While a trainer could cause training to occur without obtaining a student's explicit permission, effective training begs the cooperation of the trainee, regardless of how involuntary or unconscious it may be.

Just as a manager directs the activities of those managed to accomplish an objective, a trainer directs the activities of those trained to instill some targeted knowledge, ability, or behavior. Whereas the direct beneficiary of the manager's work is primarily the organization, the direct beneficiary of the trainer's work is primarily the trainee. Of course, it follows immediately that benefiting the trainee benefits the organization as well by increasing the potential value of its asset. The trainer's role is to increase the potential value of those trained, whereas the manager's role is to deliver actual value through the activities of those he manages.

When we think of good trainers, we consider the value of what is trained in addition to how effectively it is trained. The trainer's just reward is his recognition of the achievement of learning by his student. An ideal trainer optimizes effectiveness by adapting to the needs of his student; by so doing, he expresses the utmost respect for his student and his mission. Said another way, an ideal trainer is a student of his student's learning processes.

In contrast, a bad trainer often either trains the wrong stuff or attempts the right stuff ineffectively. The bigger problem of a bad trainer is habitually failing to observe his own shortcomings or to adapt his methods. Most bad trainers fail to observe or respond adequately to their student's responses to the training they provide.

Good, effective, and intentional trainers respect their students by adapting to their needs.

****

While the roles for each of these four distinct leadership characters vary in certain aspects, all do share a fundamental responsibility for the good and well-being of those they lead. This responsibility is common to all leaders; only the motivation and methods vary according to the particular leadership role being played.

Our Follower Characters

We next turn our attention to the "object noun" names, those of our would-be followers. While these characters share many common traits, we first focus on the distinct attributes implied by the names "*student,*" "*subordinate,*" "*dependent,*" and "*dog.*" Your dog will manifest aspects of each of these character roles in his relationship with you.

The Student

Consider the word, "*Student.*" Do not be confused by the too-frequent misapplication of this word to the undermotivated inhabitants of many of our mandatory schools. The true student's role is not a passive one.

An ideal student is an active seeker of enlightenment who recognizes the value of being trained and strives to maximize his learning. To be an ideal student with these attributes, one must possess a higher intelligence than do our canine friends. When we seek to train humans, an enlightened desire to learn for the sake of it is an enormous help.

Do not expect this help from the dog you are attempting to train. Your dog's motivation is to enhance his expectation of security and comfort by pleasing you. He is not seeking enlightenment; he is seeking baser rewards. Human students often also share such less lofty motivations. These are not bad motivations; they just are not the most compelling ones.

A dog's motivation to learn is typically simpler and less intense than a human's. Nonetheless, your role as an ideal trainer is to motivate your student to embrace learning what you seek to teach. If you are successful in this, your reward will be an easier, more pleasant, and more effective training experience.

The Subordinate

Our next follower character name, *"Subordinate,"* is derived from a word denoting a ranking of one thing below another thing, in the context of some ordering. At issue: By just which attributes are the entities ordered? In the attribute of height, for example, many leaders would be subordinate to people they lead. We all know of situations where certain bosses are subordinate to those whom they organizationally supervise, when ranked according to attributes like integrity or intelligence.

Consistent with most common interpretations of the word, possessions are subordinate to owners, students are subordinate to teachers, and employees are subordinate to their managers. However, can you readily remember who the owner of the racehorse Secretariat was? Can you name one schoolteacher of Albert Einstein? Who managed Bill Gates in his first job? The relationship implied by this noun "subordinate" is temporal and based on the specific criteria of the ordering.

In this book, a subordinate is one who by definition of an organizational structure takes direction or instruction from another, to whom he is said to be subordinate. Our use of the term implies nothing about one being better than the other.

I intend to use the word "subordinate" freely in reference to those who report in an organizational sense as well as about the pets we own without concern for misusing the term or confusing the nature of the relationship. Beyond this limited use of "subordinate," it is good practice to reflect occasionally on exactly what this word means and what it does not mean and under what circumstances the concept of subordination is even appropriate in your managerial life. Fortunately, for our immediate purpose, subordination issues should not provoke such worrisome concern when working with our canine pets.

Obvious attributes sought in an ideal subordinate include things like compatibility, ease of communication, and ability to get what you expect with little hassle, as well as only a minimal need for you to have to clean up after him. It is strikingly similar to what we seek in an ideal pet, isn't it? Of course, there are substantial differences, but if, as managers, we are able to develop our workplace subordinates toward this ideal, we should be capable of doing so with our pet, using many of the same techniques. Ideal managers develop ideal subordinates.

The Dependent

Like the word "subordinate," the word *"Dependent"* is quite sensitive to the context. Unlike "subordinate," "dependent" does not imply a ranked order. In fact, a dependency may be mutual, often without any intention by either party to create a dependency.

A dependency relationship can only be established by the one choosing to provide for the dependent. One cannot become a dependent without a caretaker enabling the dependency. Once dependency is established, the caretaker (and not the dependent) carries the ethical burden of responsibility, because the caretaker established and enabled the dependency. This ethical burden is important to consider before choosing to take on any dependent, especially one as dependent as a dog. While you may take on a dependent with the hope of achieving a benefit, there is no guarantee that any benefit should come of it to the caretaker, beyond the pleasure of having given good care.

When we consider the ideal dependent, if there is such a thing, the ideal is approached with decreasing dependency. As ideal caretakers, both for our own sake and for that of our dependent, the less dependency we instill in an object of our care, the better we serve that object.

The Dog

As our last and perchance most germane follower character name, let us consider the word, *"Dog."* Dogs embody many attributes of our other object words. In adopting them as pets, we acquire the prerogatives and responsibilities of an owner; we make them our dependents by assuming the burdens of a caretaker. They are our subordinates, and we are their managers. We intend them to be our students in spite of their lacking the self-motivation needed to be true students, autonomously seeking enlightenment. Dogs are naturally motivated to please us, albeit even if only for their own selfish purpose of ensuring the security of our favor.

Their motivation to please us, coupled with our knowledge, desire, and ability to adapt, empowers us to train them.

Throughout a rich history of relationships between humans and canines, the word "dog" has come to have many meanings in our human languages, often with richly diverse nuance. For example, to "treat like a dog" alludes to mistreatment, while "the life of a dog" connotes one of lazy luxury, though perhaps a life over which one has little control. To "dog" something suggests persistent pursuit, while "putting on the dog" means indulging in a showy display of high style. "Dog" is synonymous with "man's best friend," but most would wisely refrain from referring to a best friend, especially a female friend, as a dog, although the admiring moniker of "sly dog" is usually considered a compliment with male friends. As humans, we have certainly developed a fantastic array of images regarding this canine species with which we have become so enamored and engaged.

What I think distinguishes the word "dog" most remarkably from our other object characters is the special sense of nonjudgmental pleasure we so often derive from our image of an ideal dog, particularly when contrasted with our images of students, subordinates, or other dependents. I intend to exploit this perception of the favorable persona we so magnanimously confer on dogs as I pursue topics of leadership related to training. Never mistake my use of the word "dog" as pejorative. Think of the word "dog" as a reference to a best friend for whom you have important responsibilities to give care, manage, and train. Done well, you will develop a best friend as you embrace your responsibility to lead him to be what you want him to be.

Part One

SECTION TWO

Key Motivations
and Concepts

Why Train?

Pursuant to any leadership role, there are many excellent reasons to train. While some reasons for training may be for your own benefit, the most noble of reasons are those that benefit your student. Of course, such distinctions of beneficiary are unimportant because, as an owner or manager, what is good for your student is also good for you.

As a good leader, you train because you *should* train. In this study, we classify four distinct reasons for good leaders to conduct training:

- compatibility

- utility

- education

- pleasure

Compatibility

Managers train to cause behavior that is compatible with the behavioral preferences of those leading the organization they serve. This is typically the first training priority, because some modicum of compatibility is needed to enable an effective training regimen.

Rather than teaching new skills, most compatibility training entails discouraging some natural behavioral inclinations of the student that leadership finds inappropriate. In a human management role, instilling the basics such as codes of conduct, dress standards, working hours, and general work rules falls under this reason for training. Another common form of compatibility training is for safety, which seeks to improve the compatibility of the student with aspects of his environment that might otherwise prove dangerous to his health and comfort (or to that of others).

In your role as dog owner, you want to train housebreaking and good manners to improve compatibility. You likely will want to address things such as separating where and how he obtains his food, because most people would prefer not to share their dinner table with their dogs. Additional compatibility requirements for dogs indicate training to discourage intolerably rough behavior like jumping up, biting, and so on: behaviors that are incongruous with the interaction preferences of the society in which he lives.

Utility

Managers train to enable those they lead to perform activities that will serve the organization and thereby help subordinates satisfy the reasons that they will continue to be employed by the organization.

At work, if you want the phone answered, you train your receptionist to answer the phone the way you want it answered. If you need product parts assembled in a certain way, you train your factory workers to do it that way. If you want the convenience of having your dog bring you your newspaper, you must train him to fetch it and bring it to you.

Managers train to increase utility, primarily to satisfy their desires to obtain useful work. While doing so, they also improve their student's ability to perform useful things that justify keeping him around. While training for increased utility may seem selfish on the surface, it also benefits the student, assuming that he stands to benefit by remaining in the organization (or household) doing the useful things that you teach him to do.

Education

Managers train to instill knowledge that will empower the student to learn. Educational training develops the student's conceptual foundations and thought processes. It instills context for reference in subsequent communications or training.

If your student aspires to become an engineer, you first educate him in science and mathematics. If he desires to gain competence as a musician, you first educate him in concepts like rhythm, measure, notation, tone, and the various characteristics of musical instruments.

Training for the purpose of education is more about developing the student's ability to achieve learning than it is about instilling specific skills.

Do not mistake education as merely altruistic training. Education is often an enabler for other training that you will want to perform. Your ultimate goal when educating your dog is to instill in him an expectation that responding compliantly to your leadership cues will always result in good things for him. This must remain your key educational theme in all training-related communications.

Pleasure

Managers and owners train to satisfy their own desires for exerting influence on others. As with so many other human endeavors, we often train simply *because* we can train. People relish the ability to change and control the things around them. Like skipping a stone across a pond or yelling into a gorge to hear the echo, humans find it is extremely satisfying to cause another object, especially another intelligent creature, to respond positively to their direction. Actually, dogs do so as well, which helps them enjoy their interactions with humans all the more.

In our workplaces or educational institutions, many of us have seen managers and trainers exert inappropriate demands simply for their own pleasure. We may have resented bosses who have made such selfish demands on us just because they could. As sensitive and enlightened managers, we know better than to attempt to train our human charges to jump through hoops or engage in other unnatural behaviors at the snap of our fingers just to satisfy our selfish desire to control.

Happily, this is one area wherein the training of our pets is subject to fewer constraints than we must exercise in our professional lives. We may rightfully delight in training our pets to do silly tricks without the ethical considerations that should prohibit doing so with human subordinates.

Because we are their caring owners, we reward our dogs with meaningful treats and lavish praise for amusing us. We give them pleasure through our recognition of their success in the silly tricks we ask of them. Dogs derive a sense of comfort based on how pleased we seem with them. With the proper education, pleasing his owner equates in the dog's mind to better food, more loving care, and greater confidence that his owner will tend to his needs and desires.

Dogs perceive the praise and other rewards we give for their performance as confirmation of their being in our favor. People do too, but as a matter of dignity, people have far more concern about what they are asked to perform to gain such favor. As good managers, we should know that human charges are most likely to perform selfishly demanded activities out of fear of losing favor and all that comes with it. For your dog, however, it is an opportunity to improve his lot in life.

While you have more latitude in selecting training objectives with your dog, always strive to conduct training in a way that is respectful and fun for your student as well.

****

Each purpose for training is natural and proper in the right context (although some may be inappropriate in certain situations). Train within the prerogatives of your role. Before attempting any formal training activity, be sure that you know the results you wish to achieve. As we proceed, we will explore in more detail the techniques that are appropriate to each of these four primary purposes. For now, the main thing is to understand that there are four different purposes for training and to recognize the importance of knowing which purposes are in play when you seek to train. In order to provide good, effective, and intentional training, consideration of your purpose and your student together must drive your approach.

Communication Paradigms

We next consider the nature of communications, a vital component of every relationship and one especially critical in leader-follower relationships, such as when managing or training.

All intelligent creatures have an ability to communicate with others within their species and, often, with other species. As an experienced manager, you likely already employ most of the communications concepts that we will review here. However, as you pursue dog training, you will encounter communications challenges not so often encountered in the workplace or with others of your own species. Because effective communications tailored specifically to the student and the situation are so crucial to providing training that is good, effective, and intentional, we will expound in this chapter on some important aspects of communications.

We start this study of communications concepts with a couple of abstract yet simple intuitive definitions:

- *Information* is the base substance on which intelligent creatures exercise their intelligence.

- *Communication* is the transfer of information from one intelligent creature to another.

Communications enables training, and one might even argue that communications actually causes training of some form, whether intended or not. While our focus is on training that is the consequence of intentional communication, we must not overlook the perils of unintentional training that result from careless communications, and so we will emphasize that message as well throughout our study.

In order to train properly, we must communicate complex, descriptive information about the subject matter we want to train as well as provide motivation to receive and accept our instruction. Effective dog training includes the additional challenge of communicating with an intelligent creature that lives in a vastly different experiential context.

Important communication concepts that we will cover in this chapter include the following:

- *channel*: the conduit or media for transferring information

- *mode*: the direction and interactivity of information flow

- *tone*: the packaging of the information

- *style*: the behavioral interaction patterns when communicating

Careful and precise use of channel, mode, tone, and style can improve communications effectiveness in any situation, including (and especially relevant for our purpose) when attempting to perform good, effective, and intentional training.

Channels of Communication

A *channel* is a conduit through which information travels. Putting aside the more primitive senses of taste and smell, there are three sensory channels through which humans and dogs can both communicate at a level sufficient to conduct training. These channels are visual, aural, and physical contact.

The Visual Channel

Technically, the *visual channel* is the broadest; it allows the most information to be communicated simultaneously. A picture is worth a thousand words, so to speak.

One noteworthy characteristic of a visual channel is that it is the receiver rather than the sender who selects what he observes. Whenever attempting to employ the visual channel to initiate communication, you must first catch the eye of your intended receiver.

The visual channel lends itself well to sustaining awareness of information over time. A traffic light is a good example of this. While a changing light may catch your eye and alert you, the fact that it continues to be red is what encourages you to sustain your stop more than a transitory signal would do.

Visual cues can amplify any verbal or physical message, just as a nod or headshake amplifies a spoken "yes" or "no," just as a stare-down from a manager forcefully amplifies a verbal chastisement, or just as a friendly gaze enhances a handshake. Visual channel communications can also attenuate an intended message, either unintentionally, such as when a manager looks away from his subordinate while attempting a sincere message of praise, or intentionally, such as when he chooses to look away in a unilateral initiative to lower the level of conflict.

The visual channel is an excellent conduit to communicate positive feedback, especially to those actively seeking it. While you can effectively deliver strong disapproval with eye contact, be careful, because if you communicate negative content too often through this visual channel, you are likely to weaken your ability to use it as your subordinate begins choosing not to participate in eye contact with you.

The Aural Channel

The *aural channel,* by comparison, is typically more imposing than a visual channel. While one may look away from the sender, closing down one's hearing to an auditory signal is much more difficult. Additionally, because the aural channel does not require the intended recipient to first target the signal source, the sender has more control to initiate communications through sounds rather than by visual signals alone.

Like the visual channel, the aural channel is useful for communicating highly detailed information, at least to those with skills adequate to interpret the message being sent. One significant difference between the channels is that aural communication tends to deliver information serially and in the sequence established by the sender, whereas visual channels tend to deliver more information in parallel, while typically leaving the sequence of recognition to the predisposed interests of the recipient.

The Physical Channel

The *physical channel* is the most immediately demanding and imposing of the three channels. It is virtually impossible to ignore, and it is the most sustainable. For example, a physical restraint like a road barrier offers less choice and is less yielding than a red traffic light. However, unlike the senses of vision and hearing, the physical channel is far less suited to delivering any but the simplest information. In most forms of intentional training, the physical channel is best used to reinforce other information being sent, rather than as the primary medium.

****

The visual, aural, and physical channels each have their best uses. When communicating intentionally, all channels in play should work to reinforce the same message. Conflicting channel information, such as visually observable body language that is out of sync with a verbal message, clouds clarity. Optimize your communication effectiveness by selecting which channels you will use and when and how you will use them.

Modes of Communication

Between any two communicators, information is transferred as "input" (receiving) or "output" (sending). A "communications session" is a sequence of information input and output events.

We have three distinct communication *"modes"* available to us: the *"broadcast mode,"* the *"interactive mode,"* and the *"observing mode."* You can use any of these modes with any of the above channels, and, as with the channel, the mode you use can greatly influence the effectiveness and efficiency of the communication.

The Broadcast Mode

The *broadcast mode* typifies what telecommunications professionals would call asynchronous communication. Some experts in that field refer to the broadcast mode as "send and pray (that the message gets received as intended) technology."

The workplace office memo is a typical example of the broadcast mode. On the surface, the broadcast mode may appear to be the most efficient way to send information from one place to another. However, because the broadcast mode is purely one-way communication, it leaves the sender blind to the reaction of the intended recipient. Most written communication employs this broadcast mode, unless broken into short segments interactively delivered.

The broadcast mode is best used to communicate information that the sender expects to be readily understood or in which he has only modest interest in the reaction of the recipient. The broadcast mode has serious shortcomings for most training and many management purposes because it must presume the intelligence and receptivity of the recipient. Despite this, the broadcast mode is frequently used for just such purposes, possibly because the sender has, even if unconsciously, placed more value on the ease of communications rather than on its effectiveness. Of course, sometimes the broadcast mode may be the only practical choice, as in the case of authors trying to transmit their messages through books.

The Interactive Mode

The *interactive* (or *synchronous*) *mode* is more complicated and seemingly less efficient than the broadcast mode. On the other hand, it is much more reliable for ensuring that the message is indeed received as intended.

Communications sessions can span a spectrum of degrees of interactivity depending on the bandwidth of the channels and the receptivity of the participants to receive feedback (sometimes called "interrupts") from the other. The smaller the amount of information transmitted before obtaining and processing feedback, the more interactive is the mode.

An example toward the lower end of interactivity is Internet text messaging. While sending text uses a narrow and single-directional information conduit, the brevity of each burst of information before accepting feedback can keep the dialog interactive. On the high end of interactivity is a face-to-face conversation where the channel bandwidth includes visual, aural, and possibly physical communication. The richness of voice tone, facial and body language expressions, and perhaps even a physical touch such as a warm handshake or a gentle pet reinforce message content much more than simple text can. This is especially true when all participants are fully engaged in sharing information. Even if some are not fully engaged, one can still acquire valuable information by observing that lack of engagement in the course of an interactive session.

When significant questions of comprehension or receptivity exist, the interactive mode is by far the best mode for delivering important information. On the other hand, if your intended follower's level of comprehension or receptivity means little to you, you should probably minimize the amount of interactivity, as it is unlikely to promote pleasant or effective communications.

The Observing Mode

Our third mode of communication is the *observing mode*. Unlike the previous two, the observing mode does not place the manager or trainer directly in a transmitting role, but rather, in an active receiving role. Even so, the observing mode can cause information to be transmitted both ways.

Once any channel is opened, it begs communications to take place. A quiet open channel does not stay quiet for very long. The real power of the observing mode is that it virtually forces transmittal of information from the observed to the observer, typically information that is more spontaneous and less packaged by the sender. Through persistent listening, a leader can obtain information that will enable him to increase his leadership effectiveness while at the same time broadcasting an interest that is likely to stimulate his follower to send even more information.

Although the observing mode is the most powerful mode for obtaining information, it is also the most difficult, especially for so many managers and trainers who think of themselves as take-charge action-oriented individuals, because it demands disciplined patience and abstinence from transmitting. Indeed, while quiet observation can be agonizing to sustain, the longer silence is sustained, the greater the amount of information that is obtained. Sustain to obtain!

Tones of Communication

"*Tone*," as the "gift-wrapping" for the content of your intended communication, offers many options for packaging the message you intend to send. Choosing and using the right tone is a prerequisite to enabling effective communication of your message.

Tonal characteristics and the information they convey are often discernable, even when the meaning of the embedded message is not. Because receivers of a message usually perceive tone much faster than they hear specific words or see details in an image, the tone you use may determine whether your intended receiver will even choose to receive your message.

Elements such as brightness, volume, and force of contact define the tone. Sharp words become sharper or softer with changes in the volume of the delivery. Visual images take on additional significance through color, brightness, and animation. These characteristics combine to create the overall impression that conveys a message at least as powerful as does the embedded information.

As with channel and mode, choose your tone intentionally to complement the information you wish to send. If you want gentle behavior, use a gentle tone when requesting "Gentle!" If you want a subordinate to approach or submit when you issue a "Come!" command, package your command using encouraging and inviting tones to lessen the negative perceptions often surrounding the imposition of such commands. Loud delivery is generally unnecessary because, even more so than people, most dogs have excellent hearing, especially when they want to hear.

Styles of Communication

We conclude this chapter on communication by considering five styles of communication useful for managing or training. These styles are labeled direct, indirect, reactive, reinforcing, and combative. Certain styles may be preferred or disdained by different trainers and students based upon personalities and the situation. The most effective trainers consciously choose their communication styles more according to the student and the training situation than because of their own innate preferences.

The Direct Style

The *direct style* is short and to the point. It is the style of clear, singular purpose and unambiguous meaning. Words or other components of the communication are presented without attempting embellishment or buffering. The positive attributes of clarity and efficiency make it most powerful for issuing directives and for reinforcing training.

An unfortunate downside of the direct style is that it sometimes conveys a seeming lack of patience or respect for processes or feelings. Depending on the intended recipient, creating such an impression may weaken receptivity to the message and may even elicit combative reactions.

Another disadvantage of the direct style is that it cannot easily be used to introduce new concepts, because it requires the message to be understandable without embellishment.

The Indirect Style

The *indirect style* is characterized as one in which the sender offers multiple threads advancing the intended message without directly stating it.

The indirect style is especially valuable for teaching new concepts when there may not be a direct way to explain your subject matter using terms your student already understands. Since the indirect style requires your student to integrate your complete overall message from multiple threads, it often results in a more deeply internalized reception. Furthermore, by intentionally breaking the intended information content into multiple threads, individual threads can be delivered in a way that allows the sender to observe the reactions of his listener as he communicates each thread. This in turn enables tuning delivery of subsequent message threads with benefit of such observations to promote a more effective overall communication.

The Reactive Style

The *reactive style* is useful to instill associations of consequences with observations. It requires operating in the observing mode, waiting for the student to display a behavior, and then reacting immediately in encouraging or discouraging ways to coax the student toward desired behaviors. The key to success with this style is to observe very actively and to provide with appropriate intensity immediate consistent feedback to observed behaviors.

The Reinforcing Style

A variant of the reactive style is the *reinforcing style*. The difference is that the reinforcing style ignores all behaviors except specifically desired ones, which are rewarded quickly and strongly. The power of the reinforcing style is that it does not discourage or untrain good behaviors that just happen not to be exactly those being solicited at that moment.

The Combative Style

The last communication style we consider here is the *combative style*, a variant of the reactive style characterized by confronting the student rather than encouraging him. It is the big "No!" presented in a barrage of negativity. While it is effective to discourage unwanted activities until a desirable one appears, it is usually not much fun for the recipient, so use it in small doses and change to a reinforcing style at the instant the unwanted activity ceases.

****

No single communication style serves all management or training situations well. Participants in communication usually have preferences in the style they transmit as well as receive information. The ability of a manager or a trainer to reach beyond his preferred transmittal style and to adapt intentionally to the preferred receiving style of his subordinate often determines his effectiveness as a leader. Even a dog knows that he must tune his naturally preferred communication style when soliciting the favor of his master. To serve as his leader, you must be even better at adapting your style to him.

****

Effectiveness in the context of any leadership role could be defined as how well one's communication influences intended followers to act according to the leader's purposes for sending it. Communicating effectively with intelligent creatures requires a blend of channel, mode, tone, and style that is appropriate to the information content, the recipient, and the situation. Strive to develop the skill to customize the packaging and delivery of the information that you send. This will help you enormously when training your dog every bit as much as it does when managing your people.

Consequences, Expectations, and Value Systems

We next consider three familiar concepts essential for creating shared visions with our followers about what constitutes good behavior and what constitutes bad behavior. These are "consequences," "expectations," and "value systems."

A "*consequence*" is the result of a causal action; it does not stand alone. Students must recognize them as results of identifiable causes to have any effect on training. Intentional use of consistent consequences by a trainer accelerates learning while making the process more enjoyable for both, whereas haphazard consequences make achieving intended training goals nearly impossible. Once you understand whom and what you want to train, nothing will affect your ability to provide good, effective, and intentional training more than the skillful employment of effective consequences.

The effect of any consequence that a trainer provides depends upon the student's perception of it, which is not always the same as the trainer's perception. One must consider, for example, whether the anticipated consequence affects life itself or some important quality-of-life issue in the eyes of the recipient or whether it is perceived to be of little significance. Is it a big treat, such as a million dollars in cash or a large bone with fresh raw meat? Is it a small treat, such as a piece of rich dark chocolate or a gentle pat behind the ears? Obviously, both the significance and desirability of a consequence can change drastically, depending upon the intended receiver.

In order to be an effective training tool, a consequence must be perceived as clearly desirable or clearly undesirable by the student. Unfortunately, sometimes consequences manifest as a confusing mixture of desirable and undesirable outcomes entangled as parts of the same consequence, like getting to go to an exciting amusement park with a rotten cousin. Mixed consequences lead to unpredictable motivational effects. Avoid them.

****

Moving on to our next term, "*expectations*" are conceptual associations of specific consequences with specific causal actions. An expectation exists uniquely in the mind of the intelligent creature that possesses it. Behavioral training consists of instilling expectations of consequence to such a degree that these expectations become the rules by which the student makes his own behavioral decisions. Deeply embedded expectations drive personality.

An educated student is one who has learned a large number of expectations, that is, many rules of the "if this happens, then that will happen" kind. Note that an educated student is not necessarily an intelligent student. A highly intelligent student is one who can string together long chains of individual expectations to derive reliable predictions of outcome from causal actions that may be far removed from the eventual consequence. Intelligent students may be educated, but educated students are not necessarily intelligent. Your dog may become highly educated through training, but there are natural hard limits to increasing the level of his intelligence.

Given that our goal in training is to influence behavior, we must instill strong expectations, always working within the limits of our student's intelligence.

Expectations are strongest when they have the following characteristics:

- **Simply Formulated**

Complex formulas to achieve consequences require high intelligence to have an effect on behavior. The simpler a formula for achieving a consequence is, the more apparent the expectation is, and so the effect of the expectation on behavior is greater.

- **Imminent**

The sooner the consequence is expected to occur, the stronger the effect of the associated expectation on behavior. The timeliness of consequences is markedly more important for less intelligent students.

- **Reliable**

Surprise consequences for the same behavior dull the strength of an expectation. This is why always rewarding desirable behavior and reprimanding undesirable behavior is so important. An expected reward that is missed is perceived as a reprimand, and a missed expected reprimand is perceived as a reward and, in either case, is counterproductive to good effective intentional training.

- **Predictable**

Multiple experiences of similar consequences for similar actions strengthen the individual expectations much as a woven fabric is stronger than its individual threads. The more probable it is that a specific known meaningful consequence will occur in response to a specific known behavior, the stronger the expectation will be.

****

Our third term, *"value system,"* is a collection of expectations that drive autonomous behaviors in intelligent creatures. Good behaviors per the value system become defined as those associated with an expectation of good consequences. Bad behaviors become defined as those believed likely to incur bad consequences. The range in desirability of expected consequences differentiates the good behaviors from the very good and the bad from the very bad in the mind of the student. My personal observation is that dogs tend to follow their value systems at least as well, if not better, than humans do. (Perhaps this is because they just have simpler value systems that are easier to follow!)

When training, it is natural to strive to instill your own value systems in others. This is fine within the prerogatives of your role relative to that of your student. However, when doing so, you must remain aware that while you may understand an expectation in your own personal context, the different context of your student's interpretation of the consequences makes it potentially quite a different expectation in terms of desirability or strength. To instill a shared value system in a student, you must first understand how your student perceives consequences.

Shared value systems ultimately enable coexistence and cooperation. A key training responsibility of any manager is to align the value systems of his subordinates with those of the organization, at least those expectations related to behaviors affecting the organization.

When training your dog, your ultimate goal is to develop his value system so that he defines his own good and bad behavior according to what you want or do not want him to do. That is the most powerful result you can ever hope to accomplish through training your dog.

Rewards and Reprimands

Rewards and *reprimands* are special forms of consequence differentiated by the property that each is an unambiguously desirable or undesirable event in the perception of the student.

Strong expectations of unambiguous consequences that are meaningful to the beholder are those most likely to influence behavior. In this chapter, we will begin to study techniques for employing these two very special forms of consequences to build relationships, to encourage or discourage certain kinds of behaviors, and to introduce new skills.

We start with a caution that some rewards may not be actually good for the recipient. Examples of this unfortunate phenomenon abound. A factory supervisor suggesting, "I see you have been working very hard; go take an extra smoke break!" to a worker with a chronic smoker's hack, or a sales manager exclaiming, "Great week! Let's all go out for cocktails on me this Friday night!" to a seriously alcoholic sales team are a couple of workplace examples. Similarly, rewarding your dog with a giant piece of foie gras each time he successfully demonstrates his mastery of the "Sit" command is not in his best interest, regardless of how motivating it may seem to him. When giving rewards or reprimands, you must take into account all of your roles with respect to your student. Especially in your caretaker role, you must choose rewards that are good for your student and use reprimands with appropriate care and respect.

Any intelligent creature naturally seeks what he perceives to be good for him and avoids consequences that he perceives as negative. This enables skillful trainers to align their students' value systems with their own through the use of consequences. Once this alignment happens, leaders can get the behaviors they want voluntarily, if not enthusiastically, as their followers simply go about pursuing what they see as their own best interests.

About Rewards

We first discuss *rewards,* because motivating by using a system of positive rewards is the preferred approach for any good leader. Despite the propensity of many managers toward corrective criticism, most good managers find that rewards are much more fun to give than reprimands are. Indeed, a preference to reprimand is surely a sign of a serious problem in a manager (albeit not a rare one). The good news for managers and trainers is that there are many great opportunities to give rewards. In fact, the only rewards that you must avoid giving are those that reward undesirable behaviors.

Some Common Types of Rewards

For our purposes here, we will classify reward types as *benevolence rewards, incentive rewards, acknowledgment rewards*, and *encouragement rewards*. Each type serves specific purposes and, when delivered with intention and skill, promotes your agenda for managing or for training.

Benevolence Rewards

One excellent reason for giving a reward is simply to establish your benevolence as a caretaker and to affirm your acceptance of your dependent. Reward your student just for associating with you in your preferred manner. Familiar examples from your managerial life include maintaining an open door policy and projecting a feeling of "welcome to approach" through body language and friendly conversation as your normal disposition with subordinates. With your dog, it means lighting up your face when you encounter him and praising him just because he is your dog. (I find it odd how many people offer benevolence rewards more easily to dogs than to fellow humans. How often do you see a stranger on the street walk by and offer a friendly greeting to a dog while ignoring his walker? Practice giving benevolence rewards often and widely to everyone!)

At first glance, one might question whether benevolence is technically a reward (that is, a positive consequence to a desirable behavior). In fact, benevolence rewards are positive consequences for being in the leader's presence. They teach, "Hanging out with the boss is a good thing for me!" Simple benevolence encourages your student to maintain his receptive relationship with you, which in turn helps empower you to be his manager and trainer.

Incentive Rewards

An expectation of the possibility of reward creates a sustained incentive to comply with your directives. Incentive rewards are often manifested as a carrot on a stick held out just beyond immediate reach. The sheer hope of achieving the reward is what creates a sustained incentive to reach the goal.

Incentive effects vanish as soon as the reward is given and until it is replaced with another incentive. On the other hand, if the student never actually receives the incentive reward for his good performance, he will not continue to expect to do so, and any incentive value will be lost. The incentive reward should be offered as a viable pending conditional reward and never as a tease.

As a manager of people, you use things such as possible promotions or salary increases as incentive rewards. These are the rewards expected by many for sustained good performance in the workplace. Sales contests are another example. While the participants know that only one or a few can win, if they feel any hope of winning, it usually stimulates them all to try harder and thereby do better.

Incentive rewards in the workplace do not need to be monetary. Just the fact that a manager is known to praise good performers in front of others serves as an incentive that inspires subordinates to work harder to perform well.

With your dog, a typical incentive reward might be a small food snack held in your hand until the moment when you decide to deliver the treat as an actual "earned" reward. Your dog sees the treat and expects that the reward is imminent if he continues to conform to your directions. The potential of getting a treat rather than the treat value itself is what encourages sustained attention and conforming behavior.

Just as in your human management situations, incentive rewards need not be as tangible as food treats. The actual rewards need not be large either. Quick association with the desired behavior makes a reward more effective, because it takes high intelligence to expect and wait for less immediate rewards.

When offering an incentive, you must always be prepared to withhold giving the reward if the desired behavior is not displayed. Obtaining conditionally offered rewards without meeting the conditions turns such would-be incentive rewards into benevolence rewards and loses the incentive effect.

With your dog, be sure to differentiate reward food from sustenance food. Similar to an employee's regular paycheck, sustenance food is not a reward; it is your dog's entitlement and your responsibility to provide, regardless of his behavior, for as long as you remain his caretaker.

Acknowledgment rewards

The acknowledgment reward is a powerful device for reinforcing new skills as well as ongoing good behavior. It can be a standalone reward very specific to an observed performance of good behavior, or it can be the happy culmination of an earned incentive reward. The stronger the association the student makes between demonstrating the behavior and receiving the acknowledgment reward, the more effective it is as a training tool.

As an effective manager, you likely use a gamut of prizes ranging from bonuses to elaborate recognition programs intended to acknowledge good results. In many cases, publicly complimenting a subordinate for a good result as soon as it happens provides reinforcement more effectively than some monetary rewards, because of the close temporal association and the high value of positive acknowledgments to most social creatures.

Similarly, when training a dog to perform a new trick, you should have some reward, no matter how small, ready to deliver at the exact moment he produces the desired behavior. Praise, because it is easier to deliver immediately, can be more effective for such acknowledgment than a food treat.

The importance of proximate timing to strengthen the "expectation" cannot be stated too strongly. Less intelligent students are not likely to associate any consequence with an action much removed in time. That is why many expert dog trainers recommend the use of a clicker to mark good behavior at the exact instant exhibited. When associated with traditional rewards, the clicks provide excellent reinforcement without interrupting or distracting the training process. It is similar to phone sales organizations that acknowledge success by ringing a bell in the office each time a sale is made—a far more practical form of instant recognition than immediately going out for celebratory cocktails.

Any acknowledgment reward system should be progressive, using the physical contact of petting (not in the workplace, please!) and small treats to strengthen the reward value of immediate verbal praise when warranted. Amplify verbal praise occasionally with additional rewards like special food treats or new toys to strengthen the effect of praise alone. On the other hand, do not amplify too greatly or too often, because that may weaken the range of power values that you have in your reward options, that is, your ability to have your student perceive the difference in value of one particular reward from another. Maintain a broad range of power options in your portfolio of rewards, because some acts do deserve greater acknowledgment than others.

Encouragement rewards

Rewards can and should be given in response to generally good (but not necessarily specific) behavior. In the workplace, things like company-sponsored parties or picnics are good examples. Project-completion luncheons reward the participants and associate positive feelings with accomplishment of some organizational goal. An impromptu after-work social hour or other fun activity may reinforce the team spirit of a work group after a successful day.

With your dog, always wrap up formal training sessions with a lavish assortment of praise, petting, and treats to instill greater interest in future training, regardless of how your training performance actually went in that particular session. When you do this consistently, he will come to look with happy anticipation to future training sessions.

Techniques for Delivering Rewards

In order to get the most value from the rewards you offer, you must employ techniques that support your purpose and avoid giving rewards in a way that may confuse the expectations that you intend to instill. A few important points relative to the giving of rewards follow:

Do not confuse types of rewards.

Each type of reward serves a special purpose. Maintain each type of reward as an effective special purpose tool; hone each type of reward by using it properly for its intended purpose. Avoid giving rewards that do not suit your purpose, such as unearned benevolence rewards when your purpose was to motivate better performance. Such confusion actually happens all too often, especially with inexperienced managers or trainers.

Consider typical workplace performance rewards like sales commissions or conditional bonuses. By definition, a sales commission should reward a sale, and a bonus should be a conditional reward for actually doing something extra. However, many compensation programs commonly mislabel "commissions" and "bonuses," which are nothing more than a standard part of compensation. Commissions on ongoing account activity are sometimes given to newly assigned salespeople, even when that person had nothing to do with selling to or servicing the account. Sometimes, bonuses are given to an employee as part of his annual compensation, although they are actually just a percentage of salary and not based upon anything special he did to affect the organization.

Astute managers know that if they give so-called performance incentives unconditionally, they are really at best just benevolence rewards and have the same effect as a higher base salary; they do not influence the specific behaviors they are intending to affect. Benevolence rewards are fine, but do not confuse them with incentives in which the reward is given only upon achievement of specific goals.

Similarly, do not confuse incentive rewards with acknowledgment rewards. Incentives are offered tentatively with strings attached. Acknowledgments should be generous forms of recognition spontaneously given for achievements actually accomplished.

Associate reward cues for reinforcement.

Nontangible rewards like praise or the sound of a behavior reinforcement clicker will become more powerful as your student builds an association of these as precedents for more tangible species-specific pleasures like bonuses, food treats, or petting. The easiest way to do this is to give lavish praise or (Dogs only, please!) repeated clicks of the clicker while your student is doing something he really likes such as being recognized, eating a treat, or getting his ears massaged. Simply praising your dog while he eats his dinner builds an association that strengthens the pleasure he derives from hearing your praise, even at times when tangible rewards may not accompany it. It is all about building conceptual associations. Make the most of giving tangible sources of pleasure to your student by associating them with the nontangible reward cues that you also intend to use.

Avoid rewarding failure.

If you introduce a potential reward as a conditional incentive yet give it unconditionally, you are rewarding failure. Doing so dissociates conditional rewards from their intended purpose and not just for the particular instance in which the reward is inappropriately given. It erodes the power of the incentive reward as a tool for training. If the expected condition is not met or the requested behavior is not demonstrated, just put the treat back in the jar for another time.

Reward progress differently than complete accomplishment.

When teaching new behaviors, give small rewards to recognize small steps. Progress takes continuous coaxing. Differentiate these coaxing rewards in size and delivery from the grand reward given for accomplishment of the entire goal. Use the little ones to inspire progress; use the big ones to recognize and reward performance of the entire activity.

Avoid diluting rewards.

Effective rewards are unambiguously good consequences as perceived by the recipient. When giving a reward, do not dilute it with any extraneous communication other than possibly to elaborate on why the reward is being given. Embellishing with praise and information about why you are giving the reward strengthens its power. Diluting it with neutral information weakens the intensity of pleasure from the reward, and even worse, buffering with nonpraising noises confuses the message to a point that may undo its positive effect. If you intend to reward, do so specifically and lavishly. If you have other information or training feedback to convey, do it in a distinctly separate message.

To illustrate this point, as a wise manager, you know better than to couple a statement like, "Congratulations, Mary! Here is your bonus for completing the XYZ account project with excellent results!" with something unrelated like "So Mary, how do you like my new office furniture?" or, even worse, something probably perceived as a reprimand like, "I hope you will be spending some of this bonus money on updating your professional wardrobe." Such extraneous commentary could seriously diminish the positive impact of the reward.

Similarly, when rewarding your dog, do not mix in nonreward communications. Praise and reward lavishly as close to the causal event as you can. Focus on the moment and let the intended effect of the reward be achieved. Make the good feeling last a while. Do not tarnish the experience you are seeking to provide with distracting noises. There will always be time later for other messages, if needed.

About Reprimands

The *reprimand* is the natural counterpoint to the reward. Reprimands strengthen the positive effects of rewards by further polarizing the expected consequence of an action. To serve as an effective tool, the student must perceive the reprimand as a clearly undesirable consequence directly related to the action causing it. Avoid reprimands for which the student cannot clearly associate the causal action, because these are more likely to be interpreted as personal affronts than behavior-motivated consequences. Even more so than when giving rewards, reprimands must be given exactly when needed and only when needed. A reprimand that is analogous to the benevolence reward is extremely counterproductive to nurturing good relationships.

Common Types of Reprimands

Incentive Reprimands

The incentive reprimand is analogous to the incentive reward in many respects. The incentive reprimand establishes an expectation of undesirable consequence for identified forbidden behaviors. An incentive reprimand is only as strong as the expectation of your student that you will indeed deliver the reprimand upon his exhibition of the forbidden behavior. In your role as a trainer, you have a critical responsibility to be consistent in providing appropriate reprimands when earned. Any failure of your consistency in this regard will weaken the incentive reprimand as a useful tool in your portfolio, and what is worse, when you reprimand some forbidden actions only occasionally, any association of the reprimand with its cause may become lost.

Like the incentive reward, albeit to a lesser extent, the incentive reprimand is a useful tool for encouraging sustained conformance with your rules. Also, like its reward analog, the incentive reprimand has an effect only up until the point that the acknowledgment reprimand is actually delivered. Unlike its analogous reward, however, the actual delivery of the consequence does little toward building a positive relationship. Rewards pull; reprimands push. Good leaders prefer to pull rather than push. Use incentive reprimands only as counterpoints to incentive rewards rather than as your method of first choice. Use them to teach your student to make good decisions on his own initiative by turning up the contrast between the consequences for good and bad behavior.

Acknowledgment Reprimands

An acknowledgment reprimand is a negative consequence provided in direct response to an observed undesirable action. Ideally, acknowledgment reprimands should be the result of failed incentive reprimands; they should not come as surprises, unless you are confronting a new or unanticipated bad behavior.

As with all consequences, give acknowledgment reprimands as close as possible to the offending action. Any reprimand that is delivered so late that the student does not associate the causal action with the reprimand is worse than useless.

Deliver your acknowledgment reprimands quickly, respectfully, and progressively. Start minor reprimands as gently as you can. Always retain a stronger level of reprimand as an option in reserve. A crisp scolding at the exact point of departure from desired behavior is far more effective than a larger dressing-down after the problem has gotten out of hand.

Withdrawal

A common and often effective type of reprimand is withdrawal. Refusing to provide the reward of harmonious interaction sends a strong message of disapproval. Withdrawal works quite well to discourage aggressive or otherwise inappropriate social behaviors because it precludes further interaction until the offending behavior has stopped, instead of exacerbating a prolonged conflict. A body language option for delivering the withdrawal reprimand is to fold one's arms while facing away to avoid eye contact or verbal discourse.

Withdrawal, particularly when done as an active refusal to engage, can be quite a stinging reprimand. This dreaded silent treatment is much too easy to leverage with little effort or intention. A little withdrawal goes a long way. Regardless of whether employing it to reprimand a friend, a subordinate at work, a family member, or a pet, sustained withdrawal is destructive to relationships. As with any reprimand, use withdrawal sparingly and with careful intention.

Techniques for Delivering Reprimands

Even more so than with a reward, the delivery of a reprimand requires close attention to both intention and technique. Reprimands should be unmistakable but succinct. Here are several other issues to keep in mind when intending to reprimand:

Reprimand only within the authorities of your role.

Be mindful that the limited authorities of your role may restrict which options for reprimanding are appropriately available to you. Reprimanding beyond your earned authority will only encourage justifiable challenges to it. Only give reprimands that are within your established authority to give.

Never reprimand without first gaining the attention of your student.

To communicate a reprimand effectively, you must first engage your student in a way that conveys a reprimand is in progress. Facial and body language expressions can convey much information instantly to students looking for such feedback. However, solely visual techniques for reprimanding break down whenever the student fails to engage you visually. Verbal reprimands are often more effective, because they command attention and allow instant delivery upon observation of the offending behavior.

Always reprimand in a calm and controlled manner.

Amplification of verbal delivery by raising one's voice to get the attention of the student may be useful when warranted, but sustained amplification is counterproductive. People who scream all the time have little left in reserve to signal even stronger reprimands when needed. Reprimands are most powerful as tools when they are done respectfully and in stark contrast to a normal state of comfortable harmony. Sustaining a loud volume or otherwise assaulting the sensibilities of your student makes it more difficult for both of you to return to a harmonious state.

Always reprimand with respect.

While amplification of reprimands by using physical means is almost never appropriate with other humans, it can be an effective attention-getting device for dogs, particularly when contrasted with a norm of affectionate interaction, and when done properly, it is well within the prerogatives of an owner. On the other hand, I emphasize that physical reprimands must never be of an intensity or duration that could injure your dependent or compromise his trust in your relationship. It is for getting attention only. A little goes a long way and serves as an effective method of reprimand only when it is not sustained. The true purpose for issuing any reprimand should be to change future behaviors, not to punish past ones.

Reprimands, even incentive reprimands, should never be delivered as sustained threats.

I have observed people, even "professional" dog trainers, brandish sticks, rolled-up newspapers, or spray bottles of vinegar or other irritants as sustained visible deterrent incentive reprimands. I do not care for such practices at all. They are a push rather than a pull, a tacit admission of one's inability to lead in a positive way. Such techniques are possibly appropriate only as a last resort in cessation and avoidance training, when trying to break some strongly entrenched and seriously unacceptable behavior. In general, however, they are not indicated and should not be used.

About the Use of Punishment

I much prefer to use a verbal or visual rebuke or a sustained withdrawal to provide punishment rather than physical assaults using foreign devices like rolled-up newspapers and the like. Beyond simply being more humane, the regular use of a gentle approach is more likely to empower you to control your subordinate even when external enforcement devices may not be immediately available.

One might question when, if ever, an acknowledgment reprimand should be elevated to the level of punishment. First, any punishment must be within the prerogative of your role in the relationship, and second, any form of punishment that you choose should be very likely to discourage future episodes of the behavior being punished. Because the fear of punishment does provide an incentive reprimand, the actual delivery of punishment when earned is an absolute necessity, albeit one that may strain your relationship, especially if the punishment is perceived to be beyond expectation. In students of lower intelligence unable to sustain an association of the punishment with the misdeed, the longer punishment continues, the less it serves as an effective training tool.

With humans, long prison sentences often go uselessly beyond the training purpose of a reprimand. They may be warranted as retribution for serious crimes or to isolate dangerous or likely-to-repeat offenders from law-abiding society, but it is only the strong expectation that an illegal action will result in punishment that serves as a deterrent.

With dogs, it is contrary to your caretaker responsibility to ever inflict physical pain as a punishment. Even loud dressing downs or other noncontact forms of punishment lasting more than a few seconds are counterproductive to training, because whatever actions motivated the consequence are likely to be quickly forgotten as your dog's attention turns to his more urgent problem of figuring out how to diminish his ongoing discomfort with the punishment.

****

I would now like to close this long and important chapter by acknowledging what I hope you have already observed: I wrote many more words about rewards than about reprimands. This was intentional and, I hope, effective, and, I believe, good training about the best use of rewards and reprimands as leadership and training tools.

Training Objectives and Approaches

Whether your ultimate reason for training is compatibility, utility, education, or pleasure, success usually requires attaining some intermediate objectives along the way. Each of these objectives calls for its own techniques, and as we will observe in subsequent chapters, the more complex training applications may require pursuing a long sequence of intermediate objectives, perhaps introducing with one technique, refining with another, and reinforcing with a third.

In this chapter, we explore four simple approaches that we will use throughout our study to achieve these immediate training objectives:

- avoidance and cessation

- increased conformance

- skill introduction

- conceptual association creation

While many of these training objectives are not necessarily species dependent, details of the training technique employed certainly should be. The key to selecting the proper techniques starts by evaluating what and whom you are trying to train. What you are trying to train should dictate the proper approach. Your student and your role relative to that student should suggest the finer details of the proper technique.

Avoidance and Cessation

Objectives that call for an avoidance and cessation approach range from discouraging aggressive behaviors to stopping incompatible activities like using unsuitable language in the office or soiling the carpets in your home.

Upon observation of unacceptable behavior, your first reaction before you confront it should be to reflect on why you find that behavior unacceptable followed by considering why your student is engaging in it. This will better enable you to address the root causes and possibly avoid a confrontation.

However, while this thoughtful approach may be the best long-term strategy, sometimes a situation calls for an immediate reaction without the benefit of such reflection. Here are the proper steps to achieve any immediate avoidance or cessation objective:

1. Every time the targeted problem behavior occurs, directly confront it with a crisp, unequivocal reprimand sufficiently intense to interrupt the behavior immediately.
2. Employ a *combative style* of communication while confronting the problem; withdraw from friendly association for as long as the forbidden behavior persists.
3. Force the forbidden behavior to stop quickly; avoid prolonged conflicts that may suggest a struggle rather than an appropriate assertion of your leadership role.
4. Keep calm to avoid inappropriately intense reactions that could suggest that you are out of control, but maintain dominance in all communications channels; do not relent.
5. Return to grace as quickly as possible after the problem behavior ceases, and reinforce immediately by shifting to the conformance training approach (discussed next).

Properly educate your student from the very beginning about the intransience of your use of cessation and avoidance techniques by confronting only those objectionable behaviors that you have the immediate resolve and skills to extinguish. You must win your early battles to establish a strong foundation, so prioritize your cessation initiatives to those that you are willing to work the hardest to implement. If your student learns that your insistence is irrepressible when you are employing avoidance and cessation techniques, and if he expects that you will always prevail, he will choose to comply with any new boundaries you set far more readily than if he thinks that you might eventually give in and drop enforcement. Establish early the pattern of always holding your ground, even if it is on a very limited subset of issues, because even occasionally relenting and backing out midcourse will educate your student that there are ways he can get out of the restrictions you want to place on his behavior if he will only try hard enough to find them. If you give him that bad training, no matter how unintentionally, he will, much to your annoyance, try very hard indeed.

Increased Conformance

The objective of conformance training is to encourage specific behaviors that are already known to the student. Conformance training differs from the previous approach in that it recognizes and encourages desirable behaviors rather than merely confronting unwanted ones. It is much more of a pull than a push and, as such, offers the trainer an enjoyable opportunity to demonstrate positive leadership.

The following techniques are best for encouraging conformance:

1. Coax initial conformance while avoiding undue conflict. Use a short leash, work in a confined space, and restrict possible distractions or options for nonconforming behavior.
2. Employ a reinforcing communications style. Quickly recognize and encourage conforming behavior with praise and other rewards.
3. Sustain conformance by offering incentive rewards for continued conformance.
4. Upon observing any departure from what you expect, switch to a reactive style and immediately display your disapproval in proportion to the degree and importance of the departure.
5. Adjust the tone and intensity of your request for conformance according to the importance of obtaining compliance.
6. If your request for conformance is heard, understood, important, appropriate, and within the ability of your subordinate to

perform, never relax enforcement until you achieve the conformance you expect, and then, when you do, recognize and praise your student immediately for conforming, no matter how long it took him to do so.

Employ the conformance approach as an immediate positive counterpoint to your use of avoidance and cessation techniques for things like refining good manners, encouraging staying in approved spaces, and encouraging adherence to rules in general. We will consider further details of using conformance techniques for specific goals, like training students to wait or to approach when beckoned, when we study command training in the next part of this book.

Skill Introduction

A shared history of success with conformance approaches encourages receptivity to additional training. However, skill introduction requires much more than simply restricting your student's behavior to known options. Your student must recognize that something new is required and that he must want to focus on learning it. The motivation that you provide to your student to learn is every bit as important as the specific new skills you intend to introduce, especially with dogs, because most dogs fall well short of the ideal self-motivated student model.

Unlike avoidance and cessation or conformance training, which you must do whenever an appropriate situation arises, skill introduction is best done following a formal training plan in a classroom-like environment appropriate to the skills being introduced.

Effective techniques for skill introduction include the following:

1. Ensure your student recognizes that he is participating in a learning exercise by performing skill introduction training in a regular place and adopting a formal skill-training demeanor (task-focused and highly reactive style) to foster such recognition.
2. Establish motivation. Your student should expect to be rewarded for trying to learn as well as for actually attaining mastery. (Be sure to consider motivation from your student's perspective rather than from yours.)

3. Because learning new skills requires your student to risk failure along the way, mitigate his apprehension of such failure. Sell the upside with incentive rewards; downplay the downside by forgiving failures. Quick "No!" sounds and brief moments of withdrawal from active engagement are about as negative as you ever want to get when trying to introduce new skills.

4. Present any complex new skill incrementally; break it into smaller pieces as necessary. Continuously reward progress; do not wait for complete mastery.

5. End every formal training session before reaching a saturation point to avoid frustration and to encourage receptivity to future skills-training attempts.

6. Upon conclusion of a skill introduction session, reward your student's participation in the session warmly, regardless of the level of actual mastery achieved.

Skill introduction requires much planning, observation, patience, incremental nurturing of the new skill, and persistent encouragement to continue learning. Still, few experiences are more rewarding to a trainer than observing a student demonstrate a new skill that the trainer introduced.

Conceptual Association Creation

Conceptual associations are internalized expectations of a connection between two or more things. All training objectives present the need to associate one thing with another in the mind of the student. When managing or training, we commonly create associations of actions with consequences.

Conceptual associations that reside deeply within the subconscious powerfully influence decision-making processes. Just pick up your dog's feeding bowl or rattle his treats jar around to demonstrate how powerful conceptual associations can be.

Conceptual associations are created simply through repeated observation. Training conceptual associations with intention and purpose is the most powerful approach to providing education. On the other hand, the training of unwanted associations can be difficult to avoid. Unfortunately, much training of conceptual associations occurs without intention, because it takes no forethought or conscious effort to create them.

The news, both good and the bad, is that the technique to instill powerful conceptual associations is extremely easy:

1. Gain the attention of your student.
2. Introduce a stimulus (for behavior training, ensure your student recognizes that his behavior is the stimulus by employing a reactive communications style).
3. Immediately introduce the object or event that you wish to associate with the stimulus.
4. Repeat often and consistently; the more often and more consistently, the stronger the association will become.

Regardless of what you want to train or what the level of your student's intelligence is, conceptual associations are easier to train if the stimulus and associated concept occur at or very near the same time. The lower your student's intelligence is, the more profound the need for temporal proximity for his recognition of an association. Furthermore, the lower your student's aptitude for learning is, the greater the number of repetitions are needed to instill a conceptual association is.

Note that conceptual association techniques are also the approach that your students will use to train you. Conceptual associations often just happen from repeated observations and, often, without intention by either party to train. In order to remain in charge, you must choose which training from your student that you will permit to influence your behavior. As the leader, you must learn with intention just as you must teach with intention.

Part One

SECTION THREE

Essential Techniques

Selecting Your Student

Now that we have covered the most important concepts employed in training, we are just about ready to start putting the theory into practice. For any would-be trainer, that first requires obtaining a student. While it may not always be an option, students should ideally be chosen through a thoughtful process in which the best interests of both parties guide the selection process.

Consider your managerial experience in the workplace involving hiring and training new employees. Where do you start? Well, if you are an astute manager, you start quite a bit before your new employee is even interviewed.

The reason you hire a new employee is that you want that person to do something of use to your organization. In preparation for hiring a new employee, you develop a clear mental picture of the tasks and interactions; you understand, in advance, the personality traits that you value and that will help your employee excel in the *particular* position you are seeking to fill. In your work world, you would most likely prepare a written job description detailing a list of attributes and prior experience that you want in your new employee as well as what you are willing to pay and what other accommodations or investments you may be willing to make.

As part of this job visualization process, you want to determine what training you would be willing to provide as well as what you do not intend to provide. This is crucial to the hiring decision, because it determines the knowledge that the candidate must bring with him on day one as well as, just as importantly, the aptitudes that he must possess to succeed in your intended training program.

Developing a training vision for a new employee is typically based on these questions:

- What specific activities do you want your employee to perform?

- How much do you care about the details of how each task is performed? How much autonomous latitude are you comfortable allowing in that position?

- How important are the mistakes that your new employee might make? Could such mistakes actually harm the employee or others, or are they merely an annoyance?

- What is the difficulty and complexity of the activities you want your employee to perform? Must the training be done in layers, with each layer formed on top of a previous one? Are simple motor skills sufficient, or are high levels of comprehension, social skill, or creative thought required?

Through this process, you visualize the characteristics of which people who might be able to do the job effectively as well as a clearer understanding of the many more that likely would not work out for your situation.

You next consider a variety of available candidates and research the background of each to learn about previous experience, prior training, and demonstrated skills. You do this in part because you need to evaluate how much more training will be required to bring your new employee to an acceptable performance level in the position you have defined.

Consider hiring for a relatively simple position such as a front-desk receptionist. Prior to hiring a receptionist, you would evaluate requirements of the position in terms of skills, work habits, and personality traits. As with any position, you would base your hiring decision on ability, inclination for the work, and fit of the person with others in the office. As your front-office marquee, his personality, style of interaction, natural tone of voice, and an apparent willingness to be helpful would be more important for a receptionist in a sales or service organization and perhaps less important for an organization not so needing to project a polished image. If you depend on your receptionist as the only means for covering incoming calls or visitors, prior work record issues such as attendance and dependability would be very important. If correctly routing callers requires much judgment or discretion, intelligence gains importance as a desirable attribute.

Prior to filling even so straightforward a position as a receptionist, you must first know the key prerequisites for success in that particular receptionist position. If the person you hire lacks certain skills, you may be able to train them, but if he lacks required intelligence, personality attributes, or inclination to do the work, you are unlikely to remedy such deficits with any amount of training. On the other hand, assuming that the person you hire does have the prerequisite qualities, you can greatly enhance that person's ability to perform through thoughtful training.

Turning to a more complex position, let us examine the selection of an outside salesperson for a sophisticated product portfolio. The only reason for hiring a salesperson is so that person will sell your product to customers. The specific role is to sell, to build the business, to create customer demand and satisfy it. Virtually everything else is incidental to the purpose of such an employee. Willingness to reach out and help fellow employees in the office politely, while usually critical in a receptionist, is a trait I have often observed to be lacking in many successful salespeople.

The factors differentiating successful salespeople from mediocre ones are far more complicated than with receptionists. As a hiring manager, you look for good instincts and natural engaging behaviors. You look for a presence and style that appeals, one that makes it easier to attract your potential customer. You screen to ensure the absence of traits that will repel your customer. Many basic instincts and natural traits needed for a sales position are very difficult to train. You want to hire people who already have these required attributes.

More so than with a receptionist, the skill portfolio of an effective sales person is built on many layers. While intelligence and natural energy are all minimal prerequisites, in order for your new salesperson to become effective, you must first educate him in your organization's values and the value of its product. The complete training of your salesperson includes teaching presentation techniques that have proven effective for your product, role-playing drills to overcome objections, and the details of taking a complete order in such a way that your company can satisfy the customer. In order to select the right salesperson who can become successful in your specific environment, you must screen for an aptitude to master each of these important aspects of training.

Later, you may also want to train your new salesperson to fill out activity reports to satisfy your need for such information (or perhaps for an even higher purpose). If his compliance with paperwork requirements or other such routine is important to you, then you must screen for this dimension as well. If you are an experienced manager of salespeople, you already know that few employees are more agonizing to manage than an otherwise highly successful salesperson who will not conform to immutable requirements for attention to standard routines.

So, you may be asking, what is the connection of these workplace examples with the simple task of selecting a dog?

When you go to work, you have to spend time with those you hire, but when you go home, you have to live even more closely with your dog. That fact alone suggests you should take at least as much care in your decision when getting a dog.

Regardless of whether you are getting a new employee or a new dog, there are important activities that you should perform in separate steps *prior* to acquiring any soon-to-be student:

Identify clearly what you want and expect.

Know your expectations of your student before you get him. While there may be much you can do to enhance his compatibility and ability to perform as you wish him to perform, training can only help so much.

You can only select the right student if you have a clear picture of what you expect. When selecting a dog, consider your intended purpose for him, the environment you will provide (space, access, other creatures), his size, his shedding and drooling characteristics, his grooming and exercise needs, and all the way through to the breed-specific characteristics and the natural personality tendencies that you prefer.

Respect the importance of matching requirements and abilities.

Knowing what you want is only the first part of the formula. Many selection mistakes are made due to failures to recognize gaps between known requirements and the likelihood that a candidate will be able to overcome them. Many managers and dog owners alike, distracted by the attractive qualities of their candidates, underestimate the impact of critical differences on a long-term relationship.

While a receptionist and a salesperson both may benefit from a warm and inviting personality (they should have reliable work records, acceptable ethics, and many other things in common), these are still hugely different jobs. The right person for one is not the right person for the other. Irish wolfhounds, miniature poodles, German shepherds, Labrador retrievers, border collies, Yorkies, and common mutts are all wonderful, beautiful dogs capable of showing great love and loyalty for their owners, and each could be a fabulous pet or working dog under the right circumstances. However, many environmental and personal factors determine which dogs may work in a particular situation and which may not. Evaluate each option for its fit to your situation across as many factors as possible. If need be, get outside help with your recruitment planning process by visiting animal shelters and having discussions with veterinarians and animal behaviorists. Research the needs and tendencies of breeds that interest you. Visit off-leash dog parks, talk to owners of nice dogs, and ask them about their dogs. Even if you choose to perform the wonderful deed of securing a rescue dog from an animal shelter, interview your candidate and his current caregiver closely, perhaps even on more than one occasion, and listen well.

Select your student intelligently, not emotionally.

The only reliable way to avoid having problematic students, subordinates, dependents, or dogs is to avoid getting them in the first place. It is crucial to research the background of your potential student prior to selecting him. Perform your evaluation judiciously, matching each expectation on your list with his specific attributes or qualifications.

Always finalize your selection decision at a distance from your candidate, never in his presence. Appearance, personality, and ability to engage you may well be important factors in your selection evaluation, but you must not allow these traits to overwhelm your observation of other critical factors.

Because dogs are usually far more malleable than humans to serving our purposes for bringing them into our lives, the canine selection process need not approach quite the rigor of a proper human employee selection process (unless, perhaps, you intend him as a breeder for show dogs or for highly specialized skill sets). In any case, conducting a thorough selection process is a crucial start to building a happy, long-term relationship. You owe it to yourself and to your new dependent. Mismatches in critical areas are usually impossible to overcome or accommodate. After all, the reason to get a dog is for your mutual pleasure over his lifetime. Do not unintentionally jinx it from the start with a careless choice!

The Start of Training

In order to gain insight from your managerial experience, we again return to the familiar workplace environment and consider how the training process usually starts for a new employee. Other than what is conveyed during the selection process, early training typically begins on the first day with an orientation. The purpose of this exercise is to get the new employee off to a good start and quickly up to speed doing the things he was hired to do.

The initial task of the employee orientation is to introduce such basics as the space in which he will spend most of his time and to the others working in his new organization. As his manager, you show him where and when you expect him to do work, take breaks, and get his meals. You explain your organization's vacation policies, benefit plans, and the like. Often, even before the start date, a good manager will arrange for business cards, a nameplate, or other personalization of the workspace to make the budding relationship immediately more inviting to the new employee. By the moment he appears at your work location, you have already begun your new student's education about how he will be treated.

Consider the first introduction of your new employee to his space. Without saying a word, you begin training about your organization's values. Is the space truly personal and owned by the employee, or is it shared with others? Are employees free to personalize their space, or do organizational values of conformity make it such that you would prefer he not personalize it? Are there others who share the space? Are these others equivalent in position, or does the shared space transcend organizational level? Are there places, like maybe the executive office areas, where the new person should not go? As a good manager, you know how important it is to establish your expectations of an employee with respect to physical territory.

In your first few minutes together, through a complex array of signals ranging from word choices, voice tones, nods, smiles, and other facial gestures, as well as through your style of interaction with third parties, you will quickly begin to seed the employee's expectations about how you are going to interact with him. During the course of the orientation, should a signal that you send to your student not cause an expected reaction, you likely send it again, perhaps fortified by additional information such as tones indicating concern, urgency, or annoyance, or perhaps with additional words detailing more specifics of your instruction. Depending on how your new employee reacts to your retransmission, you continue on message or again modify your signal sending patterns. What happens in these first few minutes of the initial orientation is so crucial, because it programs subconscious expectations in both of you about how you will interact going forward and, most importantly, how you will most likely attempt to lead him.

Throughout this early introduction, your employee will also convey, often in subtle ways, his comfort with the space and any restrictions placed on the use of it. Although this is useful information for a manager, some leaders do not recognize these important messages clearly or early enough, much to the detriment of the long-term relationship. An ideal manager actively listens early and often for indications of contentment from his subordinates.

During early interactions, some of the most important signals exchanged between you and your new employee are those that demonstrate individual communications styles and preferences. It is natural to think that the new subordinate is the one receiving the training from the manager and is the party more receptive to following the manager's lead in these early exchanges. However, also early in the relationship, the best managers consciously absorb training from their subordinates. They even command such training through active observation. Top managers immediately recognize signals being sent and intentionally modify their own behavior to elicit desired reactions from their subordinates. Consciously adapting to training from one's subordinate does not weaken managerial authority; rather, it strengthens the manager's power to communicate and to motivate effectively.

In many situations, early training tends to be casual, unintentional training, which often establishes the manager in a reactive rather than proactive role. Orientation activities should be an intentionally focused proactive time that a manager spends with a new employee and not simply a series of reactions to questions and issues.

Reflecting on the new employee training experience, we now extract the essence and establish three keys to launching a great relationship with any new student and, in particular, with your new dog.

Recognize that early communication sets the subconscious foundation.

Training begins with the first interaction and continues with every subsequent interaction. Because each level builds on the prior, the foundation of the relationship comes from the earliest training. You must be intentionally conscious of the signals you are sending and receptive to the signals you are being sent from the very start. Perform the start of training with careful intention and restraint that respects the fact that you are still very early on the path toward earning the prerogatives of your leadership role.

Establish yourself as a benefactor early in your relationship.

The first item of training should be to introduce your student's space and to assure your dependent that you care about him and can provide for his comfort. Establishing your identity as a benefactor from the start establishes you in a positive light as someone of value who can serve as a potential source of satisfaction for his needs. Your student's expectation that you might be of value to him encourages his acceptance of your leadership.

Establish boundaries for your student from the very beginning.

You need to know which behavioral and territorial accommodations you are willing to make and which you are not, because if you are pushed outside of your comfort zone, you will likely lose effectiveness and satisfaction with the relationship. Set and communicate your expectations about boundaries when it is easiest to do so, which is at the beginning of your relationship before any ad hoc boundaries have been established through happenstance. Of course, this requires intention, which, in turn, assumes that you know what boundaries you want. Make sure that you do.

Observe your student attentively for behavioral signals, especially those signals he issues in reaction to the signals you send. The overarching long-term goal is to develop a shared system of values (that is, a shared understanding of what constitutes good or bad behavior along with a self-interested motivation to pursue the good and avoid the bad). Start training shared values early by using a reactive style of communications. Observe your student's behavior keenly and respond either positively or negatively to everything you observe. This will begin to teach your student to associate his concept of good with your definition of good and his concept of bad with what you define to be bad. In particular, the more your student expects that you will respond in a good way to the appropriate behavioral responses that he gives to you, the more he will embrace your leadership and all that goes with it.

****

Let us now apply these three practices to the specific tasks associated with beginning the training of your new dog.

First, make the most of the early interaction opportunities to impress upon your new dog that you are useful, helpful, kind, and totally in control. Your dog's first need is to know that you will provide for his creature comforts, so be sure to obtain basic things he will need before you bring him home: chew toys and balls, collar and leash, food and water bowls, bedding, a supply of good dog food, and a variety of treats. Put in place the things you will need to constrain his movement, like barriers to the parts of your home you do not intend to share. Make sure poisons and other hazards are secure in a safe place. Read a book about child-proofing your house from toddlers; it is quite relevant. The assortment of dangerous things that both children and dogs can get into around a house never ceases to amaze.

Your dog needs a space of his own where he can just be himself with or without your presence. This space should be a secure territory where he can hang out with easy rules and comfortable trappings, like a cushioned bed or blanket and toys of his own.

The better your dog can identify what is his and what is not, the better he will coexist with you. The more that you want him to avoid off-limit spaces, the more you must communicate about exactly what space is his. It is far better to reinforce his preference for his own space than to reprimand him for being in what is not his space. Praise him frequently just for being in his space, for lying on his bed, or for picking up one of his toys.

Ownership and territory are hard-wired into your dog's natural cognitive system. Give him what he needs to feel comfortable with his surroundings. (Many dog trainers recommend the use of a crate as the center of his dog space, with good reasons. However, as I have presumed that crating is not a practice with which the average good manager of humans is acquainted, I consider further discussion of the use of crating to be beyond our scope.)

Where needed, spatial boundaries are easy to impose and enforce with just a little preparation. Behavioral boundaries require more work.

For example, when and where your dog should relieve himself is essential information for the tidiness of your shared life. (It is more your issue than his!) Your dog is not capable of addressing such matters as proactively with you as you might expect of a new employee. You must anticipate your dog's needs until he learns how to tell you of them. Praising him while he relieves himself outside because you observed him vigilantly, anticipated his need, and took him outside in time is certainly better for your relationship than screaming and chasing him out of your home midstream. While this may require considerably more observation work at first, it is a much more effective way to train.

Your dog's expectation that you will attend to the things he needs is why he defers to you in most matters, and frankly, it is what he likes most about you. Until you establish the basic educational foundation wherein he accepts you as having some potential value to him, attempting to perform additional training is futile if not counterproductive. It will appear to him as nothing more than an unearned attempt by you at domination.

However, once you earn your right to manage and train your dog by showing him your value, so much more will become possible, as your student learns from the very beginning that following your lead is the best thing for him.

The Fundamental Rule of Effective Training

Assuming that you have selected your student well for your purpose and that you have earned the empowerment to train him, the variety of subjects you can pursue is nearly unlimited. As good behaviors become the norm, you can readily grow your relationship and expand his learning by introducing new skills to him, ideally ones for which he will be rewarded. Exactly which skills you should teach depends simply on what knowledge he already has and on what you want him to learn.

Good, effective, intentional training is an ongoing process that requires frequent evaluation of what you are training (and why) and what your student needs next from you to progress further. I refer to this crucially important yet often-overlooked process of continuous adaptation as "The Fundamental Rule of Effective Training": Constantly tune your training—both content and approach—according to your objectives and your student's needs.

Observe two essential prerequisites that enable good and effective practice of the Fundamental Rule:

- You must know your objective; that is, what knowledge, traits, or skill you want your student to learn.

- You must know your student and understand what works for him in the context of training.

Employ the Fundamental Rule every day to determine what to train, when to train it, and how to train it. As you know from your managerial world, training is an investment, which implies both a cost and an expectation of benefit. The training investment indicated depends on the experience of the student, his developmental needs, and the knowledge required of him to attain the competence that you expect. A natural goal for you is to realize the maximum value from your investment in training.

Just as the proper training curriculum for a receptionist is much different from that for a salesperson, the appropriate curriculum for a family pet is much different from that for a service dog or a hunting dog. Even with a family pet, your objectives may vary. Is your pet supposed to serve as a watchdog in a household of adults or as a gentle playmate for young children? Always put your primary objectives in the forefront. Teach the foundations required to attain your most important objectives early in the curriculum and reinforce them in all interactions. If you cannot teach the dog that you intend to become a playful companion for young children to be gentle and tolerant, teaching him to sit or fetch a newspaper on command is a waste of time.

Adhere to a logical order of presentation, because until foundation material has been learned, it is worse than useless to attempt to build up a new layer; it will only result in frustration for both of you. Thoughtfully evaluate your student's level of mastery on an ongoing basis before, during, and after every attempt at training.

Consider your student's needs regarding the pace of training. Going too slowly induces boredom, while going too quickly creates frustration. Move through your material as quickly as possible without losing your student. Have your student demonstrate his mastery frequently so you can recognize his level of learning and reinforce it with appropriate rewards. One such reward is to tune your next training activity in response to his higher level of accomplishment.

When training, intentionally control your intensity so you can provide useful information to your student about the relative importance of your subject matter. When the subject matter is of great importance, such as the safety of your student or those around him, a more demanding, intense, and rigid style is appropriate, whereas when training for recreation or amusing tricks, a lighter style with less intensity is much better. (As obvious as this concept may seem, how many times have you seen parents at Little League games or pet owners at dog parks overlook such distinctions of what constitutes appropriate intensity of communications relative to importance?)

When conducting formal training sessions, make it a practice to include some old material to reinforce and reassure; some current or new material to present, drill, and master; and some advanced stretch material to challenge or excite. Start training sessions in comfortably familiar territory to reinforce foundations while evoking memories of success with previous learning. This motivates both the student and the trainer to go forward into new areas with an expectation of good results. When introducing new material, focus on achieving frequent small advances reinforced by praise and other rewards. When doing stretch activities, use a relaxed and informal style that does not expect mastery but rather, promotes continued interest, or even better yet, enthusiasm.

Each kind of training warrants its own distinct approach. The Fundamental Rule of Effective Training prescribes an intentional and continual process in which you visualize what you want and observe what your student needs and then, with these things as your guide, engineer how to achieve it. Make this rule your fundamental practice in all that you seek to teach, and you will be well on your way to becoming an outstanding leader and trainer.

A Summary of Training Foundations

Congratulations on completing the academic foundations of this training program. I hope this review of material familiar to most managers has been useful. Your leadership experience should indeed serve you well as you pursue becoming a good leader for your dog because, as a good manager, you probably already use much of what we just covered every day in your professional life.

While much about motivation, communications, and best management practices is more or less species-independent in the abstract, appropriate application clearly depends on your role relative to that of your student in what and how you teach. Looking forward to the next part of our book and the study of practical applications, we conclude this part with a brief review of key issues relative to the techniques we will be employing.

Our definition of training is "an action by a trainer that enables or effects change in the abilities and behaviors of the student." Our focus is to perform good, effective, and intentional training and to avoid the pitfalls of careless training.

When in any leadership role, you must remain mindful of your relationship with your student, because it defines your responsibilities, your authority, and the source of empowerment to perform your role. The biggest difference between your human management role and your role as the owner of a dog is the nature of your relationship. Dog ownership confers complete responsibility for the possession as well as absolute power over the dog, whereas managers and trainers of humans never have (and must never presume) such power.

Your empowerment to perform the roles of manager or trainer requires the cooperation of the intelligent creature you seek to lead. You must earn this empowerment by offering something that your follower views as desirable, because there is no reason that any intelligent creature would submit to your leadership without perceiving an opportunity to get something for doing so.

We discussed the importance of communication in training and introduced the terms *channel, mode, tone,* and *style.* These aspects of communication are even more important with dogs than with humans, because the actual words or other message content are not usually as evident to dogs.

As the leader, you should strive to communicate in a way that will optimize receptivity to your message by choosing each aspect well. Choose channels according to the purpose of your communication that will facilitate delivery. Use an appropriate mode. While the broadcast mode may often seem expedient to many managers, modes that involve observation skills (interactive and observing modes) best enable you to tune your approach to the situation and the needs of your student. The tones that you use to package your message will determine your student's receptivity to it; this is particularly important with canine students. Gentle tones are most effective for everyday purposes and encourage gentle behavior in others. Choose the style that best supports the message that you are trying to send. Be direct when giving commands, indirect and nurturing when introducing a skill, reactive with feedback when attempting to maintain cooperative engagement, reinforcing to sustain good behavior, or combative to confront bad behavior. Vary your tone and style responsively as you engage your student to provide instant feedback to him about his latest response to your leadership.

All intelligent creatures autonomously manage their behaviors to obtain what they are driven to seek. The hope of achieving desirable consequences drives what each creature considers to be good behaviors, while those expected to bring bad consequences are to be avoided. Always consider from your student's perspective any consequence that you intend to use. Consistent repeated experience receiving consequences to behaviors creates the *expectation* in a student that future repetition of the behavior is likely to result in the same consequence. Instilling a collection of expectations develops a *value system* within the student. Value systems are the basis upon which all intelligent creatures choose their behaviors when they are free to do so.

Strongly polarized consequences known as *rewards* and *reprimands* are the most essential training tools. Effective use demands intention and careful communication. Reward and reprimand with clear intention. Do not mix messages or send the wrong message at the wrong time. A missed reward that was expected is taken as a reprimand, and a missed reprimand is taken as a reward. Mixed or uncertain consequences weaken expectations and, in turn, their influence on behavior. The more your student expects a consequence, the more it reinforces your training objective when you actually do provide it.

We discussed compatibility, utility, education, and pleasure as good and proper reasons for training (as long as they are within the prerogatives of your role relative to that of your student). Your purpose for training and your role relative to that of your student determine what you should train and how you should train it. For example, as an owner, you have far more latitude when training your dog for your amusement than you do when leading humans. Enjoy it!

Goal-oriented training requires achieving intermediate training objectives along the way. Each objective requires a specific approach. Achieving avoidance and cessation of unwanted behaviors requires instilling an expectation of reprimand associated with those behaviors. Expectation of comfort and ongoing positive recognition for doing "the right things" reinforces conforming behaviors. Skill introduction requires motivation to learn, which most typically comes from an expectation that mastery of new skills will present new opportunities for reward. Instilling conceptual associations requires only the observation of two or more things together. The more often the association is observed, the stronger it becomes. Conceptual associations of actions with consequences form the basis of self-motivation.

Good training starts with goals. Know what your goals are even before you get your student, if possible. Both aptitude and attitude empower learning. Your student's aptitude is innate; his attitude is developed beginning with your first interactions and is nurtured by the self-interest of your student throughout your relationship.

We discussed the following seven guidelines to optimize your chances for a lifetime of good training results:

- Identify clearly what you want and expect.

- Recognize the importance of matching requirements and abilities.

- Select your student intelligently, not emotionally.

- Recognize that early communication sets the subconscious foundation.

- Establish yourself as a benefactor early in your relationship.

- Observe and react to input from your student within the boundaries you set from the very beginning.

- Constantly tune your training—both content and approach—according to your objectives and your student's needs.

And finally, we conclude Part One of your training program by emphasizing two of our overarching philosophies, as we move on to apply the theory to real training situations:

- Training is done best by leading. Leading is done best by pulling, not pushing. Rewards pull; reprimands push. Rewards should be the norm; reprimands should simply be counterpoints to accentuate rewards.

- Training is a two-way street. You must learn as you teach and demonstrate in your training approach what you have learned. Good leaders adapt to the needs of those who count on them for direction and training.

I confess that in presenting the academics, I have presumed that as an experienced leader of humans, you are better at adapting your behavior than is the intended object of your leadership. If this is not the case, then you must work very hard to develop this skill. Otherwise, prepare for a lot of frustration in your attempts to lead or become accustomed to being led. At least for many, this seems an acceptable option, and that is okay. It is just not what this book is trying to teach.

Part Two

PRACTICAL APPLICATIONS

COMMAND TRAINING
AND BEYOND

Part Two

SECTION ONE

Basic Command Training

Introducing Command Training

When people think of training, especially dog training, the first thing that comes to mind for many is command training. The concept of a command is quite familiar to most experienced managers. "Answer the phone!" is an example of a command that you might use with your receptionist. "Take care of this customer!" is an advanced command that you might give to an experienced salesperson. "Down!" "Crawl!" or "Roll over!" are examples of commands more appropriately reserved for use with your dog.

A command is a special form of communication that directs performance of a specific behavior, typically with an expectation of immediate and complete compliance. Commands are control mechanisms empowered by the leader's earned role as a manager or trainer and by the follower's learned role as a willing subordinate. True commands are delivered down to subordinates; peer-to-peer or upwardly directed orders are merely requests and not true commands in our sense of the word.

Each of our character types plays a special role with respect to commands. The trainer's role is to instill and reinforce these control mechanisms. An effective manager issues proper commands in keeping with his management responsibility. An ideal subordinate exhibits the requested behavior upon receiving the command without hesitation or need for further direction. A happy and motivated dog craves many opportunities to endear himself by performing per his owner's command.

As the purpose of a command is to achieve a specific response to a signal, the educational goal when training commands is to instill a direct "accept-and-perform" conceptual association between the command cue and the desired responsive behavior. What enables command training is an expectation by the student of a favorable consequence for his responsive behavior. Do not attempt command training until you have established your leadership role as a potential benefactor.

Command training usually requires the "skill introduction" technique and, in particular, the approach of selling the upside while mitigating the risk of learning something new. Once a command has been successfully introduced by associating a command cue with a behavior, reinforcement should be done using the conformance training methods of consistently rewarding responsive behavior. While you may employ a parallel approach of reprimanding nonresponsive behavior to commands that have already been learned, recognize that the reprimand is terribly ineffective as a tool for introducing most new skills.

In this section, we introduce seven basic commands. Later, we will build a more robust repertoire based on extending and combining these primitives and by generalizing the context in which they can be employed. While other books about training might present a different set of primitive commands, the ones presented here should be conveniently familiar to you from your experience in human management.

The seven basic commands are:

Look!	*(Open a communications channel)*
Stop!	*(Discontinue whatever you are now doing)*
Wait!	*(Sustain position pending further direction)*
Come!	*(Approach/Join/Submit)*
Withdraw!	*(Do not approach/Avoid/Chill out)*
See!	*(Listen/Observe/Learn)*
Show!	*(Communicate/Demonstrate/Perform)*

Much as your first interactions with your student establish the context for all subsequent interactions, the way in which you train these basic commands will establish the context for all subsequent training. Teach and maintain your command repertoire to be completely reliable.

You and your student must share an appreciation of their importance. They must become instinctual for both of you: truly second nature.

The encouraging word is that these basic commands are simple enough for both you and your student to understand, while the behaviors they demand are not far from behaviors any student is inclined to display naturally, at least on occasion. Your training challenge is to learn how to elicit the behavior you desire in response to your command cue rather than simply to let your student manifest it upon his whim.

There are two distinct facets to successful command mastery:

- You must learn to issue each command at the right time, using the right technique.

- Your student must learn to respond correctly, immediately, and consistently.

Please note the order in which I have presented these two facets of mastery; it is of significance.

In the chapters ahead, as we introduce each of our seven basic commands, keep in mind two essential behaviors that you must manifest reliably when performing command training:

- Always acknowledge and reward compliance with your command.

- Never issue any directive in the form of a command unless you are prepared to enforce it completely.

Tolerating command noncompliance weakens mastery; it trains both of you that at least some commands are merely suggestions of optional behavior. Compliance with your command must never be considered optional. If you issue a command, you must enforce it. If you cannot or will not enforce a command that you have already issued, then you must rescind that command immediately and clearly. Always!

The *Look!* Command

Consider the encounters you have with your subordinates in your organizational life. Are you the kind of manager who always makes it a point to pause and engage your subordinate's attention before giving him direction? If so, then the purpose and importance of our first basic command are probably obvious to you already.

The *Look!* command opens a conduit for communication. Its simple purpose is to get the attention of a subordinate while establishing the channel and clearing out any static. It signals intention to communicate information and directs attention to the commander as a precedent to further activity. With humans, for example, one may start a speech by saying, "Ladies and gentlemen," or open a conversation with, "Hi, Mary. Can we talk for a moment?" With a dog, just saying his name clearly and with a tone of intention is usually sufficient for the purpose.

Unfortunately, priming *Look!* commands are often carelessly skipped, thereby detracting from the effectiveness of intended communications. Have you ever watched a supervisor streaming directions nonstop into the back of his subordinate? It is not very effective or attractive, is it? The worst cases in point are when reprimands are given that way, but failing at any time to engage fully before attempting communication wastes time and usually contaminates the intended message content. The *Look!* command is well worth what may seem like an extra step.

The behavior requested by the *Look!* command is quite natural for humans as an instinctive or early-learned behavior. When you speak to or look at another person, he typically looks back at you (unless he has unlearned that behavior, for some reason). Although the return eye look may not be as natural for your dog, you can easily train it. A small food treat held in your hand will get your dog's attention. Say his name followed with the command word *"Look!"* or *"Look at me!"* while bringing the stimulus to your face near your eye. As the eye of your student meets yours, generate enough facial interest to encourage eye contact and cause him to transfer his attention from the treat to you. Once he sustains his attention on you, give him the treat by gently placing it in his mouth while encouraging continued eye contact by praising him for looking at you. Do not throw the treat, as that may cause him to disengage eye contact with you to get it. The goal is to teach him that he is rewarded for the engagement with you rather than for catching the treat.

Praising words and smiling gazes keep eye contact comfortable, but just as with your human subordinates, avoid staring, because that implies an attempt at domination and comes across as being quite confrontational.

When issuing a *Look!* command, typically the channel of choice is the aural channel, because it does not require your intended listener to be tuned in to you already in the way the visual channel does. Just call your subordinate by name in a positive tone, possibly with a few extra social sounds thrown in, depending on whom you are addressing and what is to follow. As a leader, you want a comfortable, positive response from your would-be follower to your use of his name or to any attempt to open a communications channel with him. You want to gain his attention, accompanied by a receptive attitude. Teach this by intentionally managing your tone (as he perceives tone) to support acceptance of the message you are intending to send.

Because the *Look!* command should seem only mildly intrusive to most, it rarely warrants initiation or amplification using a physical channel. In fact, physical contact should be avoided until the student has already heeded a verbal or visual *Look!* and the channel is established, unless, of course, you are intentionally seeking to startle or dominate. (Why would any good leader do that?)

Reinforce the *Look!* through frequent use in positive applications. Make it a point to catch the eye of your student every time that you give him a reward. Once you establish that attentive eye contact is a good thing, that is, a behavior that he associates with getting him something he wants, it will be easy to train any number of verbal or visual variants of the command.

Opening a communications channel should be a pleasant experience, even when the message you intend to communicate is unwelcome. Although there will be times that you must communicate unwelcome messages, there should be many more opportunities to communicate positive ones. Take advantage of these positive-message opportunities to strengthen your student's expectation that complying with your *Look!* command is a good thing. For easy practice, just command "*Look!*" to your dog by gently calling his name and smiling genuinely while offering praise to reward compliance, and every so often, use the *Look!* command as a prelude to giving him a bigger benevolence reward such as a treat.

The *Stop!* Command

The *Stop!* command demands immediate cessation of a targeted activity or behavior. For purposes of safety and control, a reliable *Stop!* is an indispensable element of any command repertoire. Mastery of the *Stop!* command provides an essential tool for establishing control when needed. It is the emergency command to issue when there is no time or desire to provide further direction (or even when you have no idea of what you want to direct beyond the immediate cessation of some activity).

With your dog, a reliable *Stop!* command enables you to perform your responsibilities as his owner, caretaker, manager, and trainer. The more powerful you can make your *Stop!* command, the better and gentler leader you can be for him.

As useful and necessary as the *Stop!* command is, I would like to raise several important precautionary issues to consider surrounding its use.

Far more so than the *Look!* command, the *Stop!* command is highly intrusive. It is often so unwelcome, because it interrupts what the subordinate has chosen to do and is actively pursuing. Too often, a *Stop!* command is improperly issued in place of or without the benefit of a priming *Look!* command. The fact that the *Stop!* command lacks the positive rapport-building qualities of a polite *Look!* also exacerbates the problem.

Stop! is not a persistent command by itself. While you may employ *Stop!* command to cause an immediate interruption of something that you are seeking to halt, do not expect the command's effect to last very long on its own. If a *Stop!* is not followed promptly by additional direction, any intelligent creature is likely to determine and follow a direction of his own, often returning to the activity he was pursuing when commanded to stop.

Stop! is the most unwittingly overused of all commands. Consider, as evidence, human toddlers, who make its sister word, "No!" among the first and most persistent words of their budding vocabularies. The fact that issuing a *Stop!* command requires absolutely no forethought contributes profoundly to its mindless popularity. One simple syllable: "*Stop!*" is all you have to say. What a powerfully controlling command it is, yet so easy to issue! Imagine if you were to issue some kind of *Start!* command without forethought or additional direction. Now that would certainly yield some quite unpredictable results. However, the behavior expected in response to a *Stop!* is clear in every context, which also helps make it easy to overuse.

Despite these concerns with receptivity, misuse, and overuse, you must develop your *Stop!* command to cause immediate and complete discontinuance of any activity that you have targeted whenever you issue it. The following describes a simple and practical way to do so with your dog. It takes only intentional focus, consistency, and persistence.

Unlike most commands, informal training of the *Stop!* command usually begins without intention, as an unplanned confrontation of some observed undesired behavior. Even before you begin formal training, you probably will use the word as a reprimand because of some situation that has arisen. This is okay in that it familiarizes your student with the meaning of the cue word, but ideally, whenever using that word, you should also employ the *avoidance and cessation* training method. The following techniques are used for this method:

- Instantly identify and address the offending behavior.

- Transmit an immediate, sharp, and unequivocal reprimand. (*Stop!*)

- Associate the command with the behavior, not the student.

- Withdraw from friendly association until the offensive behavior ceases.

- Return to grace as soon as possible after the *Stop!* command has been fully obeyed.

We apply these same cessation and avoidance techniques to develop an effective formal *Stop!* command. The goal is to make the command completely reliable in every situation, regardless of context. Achieving this requires that you learn when and how to deliver the command while at the same time developing your student's receptivity to receiving and obeying it. You must move beyond just using the command to confront bad behavior and advance to using conformance approaches to train your student to choose to stop on your command. Your training approach should strive to keep the context positive and nonconfrontational.

With your dog on a leash under your physical control, "Stop walking!" is a great place to start formal training of the command cue, because the situation is generally positive, and the context of the *Stop!* is clear. Moreover, with the leash, you also have an effective physical mechanism in place to enforce your *Stop!* command. Practice by taking a few steps forward with him and then gently issue the command cue, immediately followed by a gently applied but unyielding restraining tug while you stand perfectly still. Over multiple training sessions, progressively make your tug gentler until your verbal command cue produces the desired pause without any tug. Once your dog chooses to stop on command without physical reinforcement, reward his success by changing your training approach from that of cessation and avoidance to one of conformance training. This strengthens your student's receptivity to your command, as he comes to expect that compliance is a good thing that offers an opportunity for reward when done per your command cue.

The most commonly used delivery channel for the *Stop!* command is verbal, especially when directing a dog. The proper technique is to start with a verbal *Look!* command, followed quickly with the word "stop," as in, "*Rex! Stop!*" delivered in a firm but unalarmed tone. You could also imply a *Stop!* command just by saying, "*Rex!*" in a reprimanding tone, but by consistently using the actual *Stop!* command cue word in a steady voice, you reinforce its familiarity and power without needing to suggest even a hint of reprimand.

Tone can amplify or attenuate the effect of your command. The sharper and more startling the delivery is, the more likely it is to disrupt the status quo, but on the other hand, an overly aggressive delivery might also increase feelings of conflict or otherwise diminish receptivity to your subsequent direction.

With a human subordinate, you would likely intentionally use tone to convey additional information, and in deference to his human intelligence, you might even choose to make your voice lower and softer in order to diminish the sense of conflict often associated with a *Stop!* command. With your dog, however, at least initially, you may need to use a sharper, somewhat louder tone to accentuate the urgency of your command. Just avoid overdoing it, or you may appear to be confronting him rather than directing him.

With a human subordinate, you would normally want to clarify exactly what it is that you want him to stop, so you might even tell him why you are issuing the command. On the other hand, given the simpler mind of a dog, *Stop!* usually only works in the immediate context, and the additional noise may dilute the main message of your command.

One kind of pathetically useless noise that I have observed some people append to their *Stop!* commands that I find sadly amusing is something like "Stop, you bad dog! You are a very bad dog! Stop it! Stop it! Stop it!" and similar agitated ramblings. Such additional racket only detracts from what should be a very concise, clearly delivered, and easily understood command.

As you know, humans suffer the same distraction of purpose when confronted with such unnecessary additional noise. While certain information might be provided to focus a *Stop!* or explain why it was issued, additional negative personal commentary is counterproductive. Effective leaders avoid displaying unnecessarily confrontational behavior with their followers.

The most effective way to deliver a *Stop!* or any other command is to issue the command followed by displaying a calm expectation of properly responsive behavior. Repeat a command cue only if you believe that you were unclear with your first delivery. Provide additional enforcement when necessary, but keep in mind that extraneous sounds only cloud the message and allow that the command cue might not be obeyed on its own on the first time, every time, as it should be obeyed.

Stop! commands may be given visually as well verbally. Start with a *Look!* to gain the attention of your subordinate. Once you have his attention, associate a visual cue such as an open-palm hand raised in the stop position with your verbal command. Do be clear that your raised open-palm hand is not intended for striking. It is only an easy-to-use signal for a gentle visual delivery of the command cue. Try to avoid using any kind of confrontational cue signal for the *Stop!* command, because you are seeking cooperation rather than confrontation whenever you issue it. *Stop!* needs to mean exactly what you intend; it must never be interpreted as a signal to enter into confrontation.

Ideally, with practice, even a very gentle visual delivery such as a raised eyebrow can be sufficient for an observant and receptive subordinate.

Regardless of how gently you issue your commands, and gentler is better, you must still make it unquestionably clear that compliance with your *Stop!* command is always mandatory. Training a reliable *Stop!* requires unrelentingly strict enforcement. Any *Stop!* that is not heeded must always be enforced by whatever additional means is necessary, including, with your dog, physical restraint such as grasping his collar or using a leash and harness to provide immediate and effective reinforcement. Always persist patiently yet firmly while minimizing manifestations of anger or conflict until he cooperates. Your goal is to teach that especially when you are calm and intent, compliance is his only option.

Some dog trainers recommend use of pincher or even electric shock collars to reinforce *Stop!* commands. Admittedly, such devices do provide immediate and persuasive enforcement, and that is indeed preferable to and more effective than prolonged conflict. Personally, however, I prefer to avoid these harsh artificial devices, if possible. Much like the harshest disciplinary options that you might have available in your workplace (*hopefully not physical pain-inflicting devices!*), these are techniques of extreme resort. Try instead to encourage compliance by practicing in an environment conducive to training using the potential for reward rather than fear of reprimand as your motivational approach. Analogous to the "short leash" you might place on a subordinate performing questionably in your workplace, your goal is to restrict your dog's available options to a point where he decides to cease his pursuit of the targeted activity when you command him to stop.

In summary, these are the keys to establishing a reliable effective *Stop!* command:

- Avoid overusing the command to prevent it becoming perceived as a frequent unwelcome intrusion. Whenever possible, suggest positive alternative activities to redirect behavior instead of using the command.

- Whenever you do issue the *Stop!* command, enforce it every time all the way to a full stop (not just a "roll-through" stop). Your goal is to achieve a complete break in activity by instilling the expectation that it is his only option and, indeed, a good option.

- Under no circumstance should you ever allow a *Stop!* command to go unheeded, because to do so in any situation is to weaken it for all purposes.

- The *Stop!* must trump all other messages. Once you issue the command, any communication that does not reinforce your command must cease until the *Stop!* is obeyed.

- The more broadly you employ the *Stop!* command, the more broadly you can employ it. Use your command cues for all kinds of activities you want stopped. Instill and reinforce conceptual associations with your cues to make them familiar and applicable in a wide context.

Besides breadth of application, the other critical measure of strength in a *Stop!* command is the speed and completeness with which the subordinate halts the targeted ongoing activity. Drill with reinforcement methods to build strength. Although training the *Stop!* command may begin as a confrontation (avoidance and cessation), consistently rewarding compliance is the best reinforcement. Make the transition from him enjoying what he was choosing to do to stopping that activity on your command as pleasurable as you can for him. Always acknowledge and reward voluntary compliant stops, even if just with a praising "Thank you."

****

We close this chapter by observing two different contexts in which you will want to use the *Stop!* command. The first context is to stop activities that may be permissible under some circumstances. This is the conditional *Stop!* The second is the unconditional *Stop!* which means "*Never do that!*" This second form is a standing order that dictates perpetual avoidance. While, like the conditional form, it is taught as an immediate action command, it has a persistent effect as well when properly instilled. Most of the preceding instruction on use and techniques can apply to both situations. The following highlights the differences.

The Conditional *Stop!*

The Conditional *Stop!* is a control command given to cause a subordinate to disengage from whatever he is currently doing, even if it is an often-permissible activity. As it is mastered, the conditional *Stop!* evolves from being a direct confrontation to being an appeal to engage in a different activity. For example, in your workplace, when interrupting a subordinate from his current activity to discuss a topic of your choosing, rather than commanding him to stop what he is doing, you usually employ a gentle *Look!* command said something like a polite "Excuse me!" to engage him in the alternative activity of talking to you.

One common canine application of the conditional *Stop!* is for the safety of your dog around traffic, such as when you are going for a walk together. In the beginning, as you approach a street crossing, you may need to exert considerable force to keep your dog from walking into the street, where he might become injured. As your training advances, a light tug on his leash accompanied by your quiet command to stop should suffice, followed immediately with an alternative behavior command like "*Sit!*" or "*Wait!*" reinforced with praise for doing so. Stopping under such circumstances becomes a pleasurable cooperative routine rather than a confrontation. With time, as you approach intersections, the command is more likely to be anticipated and obeyed with only a slight indication.

Use force when you must, but always strive for easy, enjoyable, voluntary compliance as much as possible when issuing conditional *Stop!* commands.

The Unconditional *Stop!*

The unconditional form of the *Stop!*—the "*Never do that!*"—usually starts as a confrontation of some unacceptable behavior and without a moment to resolve your intention beyond halting immediately that which has started to happen. Presuming it is within the prerogatives of your role to do so, you are justified in giving an unmistakably vehement reprimand in proper measure to the offending behavior.

Your "*Never do that!*" reprimand should be intensely focused: high in amplitude while lasting only long enough in duration to cause the behavior to stop. Force the activity to stop by sending an immediate, unmistakable message of disapproval and then disengage. Little is gained by extending the duration of the reprimand unless you intend to punish, in which case I would remind you that at least with dogs, punishment is useless as a method for positive behavior modification. Extended periods of punishment or other discord send confusing messages while diminishing your attractiveness as a leader.

As with most things problematic, it is easiest to address problem behavior before it develops. Issuing a firm *Stop!* at the moment you anticipate that your subordinate is about to engage in forbidden behavior is far more effective for teaching and reinforcing the "*Never do that!*" than confronting him after the transgression is in progress. Of course, this does require your constant observation, anticipation, and follow-through. Gaining avoidance of forbidden behaviors should be well worth your vigilance, and if not, you may want to reconsider why you have determined that the behavior is so forbidden. If it is truly a *"Never do that!"* behavior, try to anticipate when it is about to occur and redirect your student's activity. In the event that he enters into the forbidden behavior, never fail to reprimand him strongly and to force immediate and complete discontinuance, regardless of the situation. On the other hand, if it is not really a *"Never do that!"* behavior, then do not treat it as if it is.

The *Wait!* Command

Wait! is the command to sustain your subordinate's patient inactivity until you lift the restriction and release him. You need the *Wait!* command in your basic repertoire, because you cannot always address everything at once. It allows you time to gather your thoughts and to organize further direction.

Indirectly, you imply a *Wait!* command by issuing a *Stop!* without giving further direction. You may have seen managers unconsciously let their organizations fall into a state of inaction by stopping one activity while failing to provide the positive direction needed to take on a new activity. Take care never to issue *Wait!* commands inadvertently; they waste time and resource while annoying your subordinates.

On the other hand, you can and should use the *Wait!* command consciously to buy time when you want it, for letting situations settle or to allow further contemplation. It is also appropriate for queuing activities such as traveling through restricted passages, for example, when sharing a steep stairway with a large dog. Dressed-up-for-human-consumption command phrases like "Would you hold the phone for a moment, please?" or "We will gladly reconsider your request for a promotion again in six months!" are familiar examples of managers using the *Wait!* in the workplace. With dogs, *Stay!* is a common variant of the *Wait!* command to request holding in place.

The *Wait!* command is different from both the *Look!* and the *Stop!* in that it does not seek to change the status quo; it seeks to maintain it. *Wait!* does not require action in response; it requires recognition of the meaning of the command and the self-discipline to sustain a position over an extended period.

As commands, *Stop!* and *Wait!* are not interchangeable. The first is a call to cease action; the second is a demand to sustain the current state of affairs. Because *Wait!* has its own meaning, it requires a unique sound to serve as the verbal command cue. Distinctly pronouncing "*Wait!*" in a calm yet firm voice works well for this purpose.

Because you can sustain a visual signal more readily than you can a verbal cue, the visual channel is a natural choice for nurturing compliance with *Wait!* commands, regardless of which channel is used to initiate them. This advantage is more pronounced with a canine than with a human because of the shorter attention span of canines. A prolonged raised open-palm hand of the visual *Stop!* command is a good method for sustaining the *Wait!* This same visual form can be used for both *Stop!* and *Wait!* because the sustained visual cues do have similar meaning.

Invoke *Wait!* commands by giving a clear intentional verbal or visual signal. Because it is a request for conforming behavior, *Wait!* is best introduced using incentive rewards and conformance-method training techniques. These are some conformance-method techniques:

- Force conformance without undue conflict (e.g., a short leash or restricted space).

- Recognize conforming behavior with praise and other rewards while indicating an opportunity for even more rewards for sustained conformance.

- Display immediate disapproval upon any departure from the expected conformance and increase that disapproval in proportion to the degree of the departure.

- Never abandon demanding conformance in a situation in which it is required.

As with most other commands, delivery of the *Wait!* should be preceded by a *Look!* in order to gain the subordinate's attention and increase his receptivity to the command. Most likely, with your dog, you will also precede it with a positioning command such as *Sit!* or *Down!*

to specify the position to maintain (ideally one that is comfortable for him).

When you first begin training the *Wait!* command to your dog, you may want to use a physical restraint or an assistant to help him sustain his position. Have the restraint already be in place before issuing a *Stop!* and then verbally issue the *Wait!* command. Follow this immediately by a sustained hand signal, followed by sustained eye contact without the hand signal, followed by looking away briefly to encourage your student to sustain the wait on his own. Move back up through these control levels as soon as his wait begins to waver. While eventually you will want a sustained wait in response to just a single transient cue, it may take several steps to get there. As with all training, judicious use of progressive reinforcement will help, and over time, with encouragement, your student will become more capable of sustaining his conformance with your *Wait!* command on his own.

Once your student understands and sustains the *Wait!* without reinforcement, drill to sustain it over longer durations and in the face of greater distractions, such as with others present or by walking away. As you are getting started, drill on duration and distraction levels separately. Once he can maintain a wait over a prolonged period or in highly distracting environments, combine and drill increasing levels of both.

Waiting can be difficult; be sure to reward it. To ensure his recognition that the reward is specific to the activity of waiting rather than whatever activity comes after waiting, reward the successful *Wait!* by returning to your student to reward him while he is sustaining his wait rather than causing him to break his waiting position to receive his reward.

It makes no difference whether human or canine; if your student expects to benefit by maintaining his wait, he will strive to do so. On the other hand, if sustained waits are rarely rewarded, they will be difficult to maintain.

The *Come!* Command

Through your experience as a manager, you know that one of the most crucial skills that you need in order to perform your role is the ability to get subordinates to join with you and to submit to your leadership when you call upon them to do so. Properly mastered, the *Come!* command serves this purpose regardless of the species of the creatures that you are leading.

Having subordinates obey your every beck is a hallmark of strong leadership but one not easily achieved. As you may have recognized from your organizational life, *Come!* may well be the most difficult of the fundamental commands to train to a 100 percent reliability level.

The training challenge begins with the fact that *Come!* is potentially a very intrusive command, especially in certain urgent situations when it is most needed. *Come!* tells your subordinate to place himself further under your control and to submit to your program for him. Such submission is neither natural nor comfortable for an autonomous intelligent creature, especially if he does not perceive a good reason for submitting.

Because *Come!* is more challenging to execute than are our previous three commands, be sure that you have trained them well before attempting to train the *Come!* command formally. When doing any kind of training, you must establish the foundations before trying to build the next level. The next success is best built upon a foundation of previous successes.

To get started on training this command, first establish a positive association of the cue word "Come" with the act of approaching. Any dog in an ongoing relationship with you will naturally approach you from time to time to get your attention. Whenever you observe that he is about to approach you of his own volition, support his approach by repeatedly saying the cue word "*Come!*" while giving praise and occasional tangible rewards upon his arrival. Because he is approaching you anyway, he does so under circumstances in which you will not likely encounter resistance to your beck, and so you will not need to reprimand his failure to comply. This enables a happy introduction of the command cue.

Establishing a pattern of successful compliance with any command, even in such an unchallenging situation, is building a pattern of success nonetheless. When training, feel free to stack the deck for success by lowering chances for failure. Just be honest with yourself and your student about what you are doing and why you are doing it. In this case, you are associating a cue word with an act of approaching in a positive context to help your dog learn to expect a positive consequence for approaching when he hears the cue.

After you have introduced the sound of the command word to your dog and have associated that it means to approach you, your next learning challenge is to get him to approach at other times when he would have little inclination to approach. This is done by instilling a strong association of his action of responding to your cue with the concept of getting a reward.

Because the *Come!* command requires an intelligent choice to conform, it is important when training to ensure success by carefully preparing your student to be receptive to your delivery of the command. One technique to use in a formal training environment is to start by issuing a *Look!* followed by a *Stop!* to interrupt any distraction, and then follow that with a brief *Wait!* before issuing the *Come!* command. This promotes conforming through a series of incrementally demanding choices. Since these priming commands are easier to effect, they get your dog into a relatively neutral situation, from which he will respond more readily to your *Come!* command. Furthermore, this sequence establishes a pattern of successful compliance with easier commands before you issue the more difficult one. It's much like the salesperson's technique of running through a series of easy questions with obvious "yes" answers before going in for the close.

An excellent practice drill with your dog is to issue and sustain a *Wait!* with eye contact (or with the help of a training partner cooperating to restrain him, if necessary). Next, display a small food treat in your hand held high (not in a giving position) while continuing to sustain the wait. Then, as you say, *"Come!"* in a firm and clear voice, change your body posture by lowering your hand to a giving position. When he approaches, give him the treat gently and praise him lavishly. Repeat this sequence many times to establish a clear contrast between the *Wait!* command and the *Come!* command. Reward compliance with each command every time.

To move up to the next level, discontinue displaying a reward when preparing to issue the *Come!* command. Start with a *Look!* and then issue the *Come!* command while maintaining eye contact and expecting compliance and then give him a hidden treat upon his approach in response to your cue. This associates the reward more closely with obeying your command rather than with the appearance of the treat. Practice frequently.

As an experienced manager, you know that you must command the obedience of your people, especially in the toughest of predicaments. On the other hand, you know better than to give orders that will not be obeyed, because doing so erodes your authority. Rather, you make it a practice to give only commands that you expect will be followed and that you are prepared to enforce if they are not. Through your relentless enforcement, compliance with your command becomes routine, because your students learn it is the only alternative that will yield good results. The same approach of judiciously choosing when to issue the *Come!* command, coupled with relentless enforcement when you do issue it, will work just as well when training your dog.

With your dog, you need the *Come!* command to be effective even in difficult situations, such as when your dog is playing with other dogs or running toward danger. In order to be adequately useful, like the *Stop!* your *Come!* command must achieve instant compliance in busy and distracting environments, even when you do not have tangible rewards available for enticement. Achieving such high levels requires persistently strengthening the command through many repeated successful performances of him deciding to conform to your direction in ever more challenging situations.

In difficult environments or with unimportant situations, take care to use *Come!* commands sparingly and with precision. Never confuse your intention by using the command as an informal summons. Always issue the command as a direct, unambiguous order and never as an optional invitation. If you are simply wondering about your dog's whereabouts or want to encourage him to come visit you, just call his name (*Look!*) or ask, "Where are you?" That will usually get him to approach without risking a violation of a command that you are not prepared to enforce. Reserve the precisely delivered and toned command *Come!* for occasions when his immediate response is expected and will always be enforced.

The *Withdraw!* Command

The more that you train and interact with your student, the more he will want to reciprocate. One outcome is that he will occasionally approach you for more training, interaction, and rewards than you may care to give, at least at that moment. Such increased desire for interaction is a good thing that you do not want to discourage (so long as it does not create unwelcome dependencies). On the other hand, as the manager, you need to control the attempts of your subordinate to control you, or you won't stay in charge for very long. The *Withdraw!* command allows you to control demands and interruptions without undoing the good effects of your dependent's desire for more interaction.

Unlike the preceding commands, the *Withdraw!* is rarely issued by saying the exact command word, although this literal form can make an effective and, to some, an amusing command when given in a loud voice to human subordinates approaching you at the wrong time. However, usually, rather than crisply commanding "*Withdraw!*" you respond something like, "Bill, I can't address this right now. I would like to get back to you a little later. How about meeting tomorrow morning at ten o'clock for coffee?"

In a response like this, you acknowledge your subordinate, you inform him that you are currently unavailable to him, you commit your future availability to him, and, ideally, you set an expectation for when that will be. Something like this works with humans the vast majority of the time. When it does not, you must decide with intention whether to yield to your subordinate's persistence or to retransmit your message to withdraw, amplified by stronger wording or intonation.

Consider the situation when your dependent is canine. Similar to a human subordinate, beyond just seeking your attention, your dog is seeking to control your actions. However, that is not within the prerogatives of his role; as his leader, you do all of the controlling. Your proper response is to acknowledge him, to inform him that you are currently unavailable, and to affirm your future availability. You do not want to decrease his desire to interact with you; you just want to suggest a different time or circumstance for doing so.

While one might consider using a *Stop!* or a *Wait!* in such a situation, the *Withdraw!* command is a distinct and better choice. The problems with the *Stop!* command are that *Stop!* is often perceived to be somewhat of a reprimand and that it is a short-term action command that presumes subsequent direction. The *Wait!* command also presumes further direction to end the period of waiting. *Withdraw!* is the basic command to tell your subordinate to go away until later, without necessarily implying a reprimand or creating an expectation that further direction is immediately forthcoming.

Begin training the *Withdraw!* command using cessation and avoidance approaches. Because your dependent is engaging you intently already, you do not need to prime the *Withdraw!* with a *Look!* command, as you should with other commands. Your immediate goal is to lower his level of engagement temporarily.

With your dog, the best way to accomplish this is to withdraw yourself from the interaction. Simply breaking eye contact, turning away, or emphasizing your withdrawal from the encounter with folded arms and persistent nonengaging posture confirms your command to withdraw. If your dog persists, look at him, say "Not now!" or "Later!" and turn away again. Because of his lower intelligence, you may need to employ stronger body language than would be polite with a human subordinate.

You cannot reinforce the *Withdraw!* command with an immediate acknowledgment reward, as you might with other commands. To do so would be counter to your purpose for issuing the command. The only way to reinforce the *Withdraw!* command is to maintain the withdrawal posture relentlessly until your subordinate ceases his attempt to engage you. If you allow him to find a way around your command to withdraw, he will learn that disobeying your command by persisting with even more intrusive attempts is indeed a viable means to gain control over you. Failure to sustain any *Withdraw!* commands that you issue in effect trains your subordinate how he can become your boss through stubborn persistence.

Once your dependent has acknowledged and obeyed your *Withdraw!* command, you may and should quietly thank him with some gentle praise such as "Thank you for understanding." or "Good dog!" as appropriate to the particular subordinate. This acknowledges that his withdrawal has pleased you and affirms his continued in-favor status while he keeps his distance, thereby reinforcing his compliance.

As you would with a human subordinate, if your dog usually responds to your *Withdraw!* command but persists in a particular situation, observe carefully for the cause of his persistence. He may be trying to tell you something that you need to know and respond to immediately. If you change your mind and drop enforcement of the command after such an observation, then that is being smart, not weak. Just be sure to communicate that you have rescinded your *Withdraw!* command by issuing a *Come!* and rewarding his compliance with that command.

In order to make the *Withdraw!* more palatable to your subordinate, always attempt to communicate the nature and duration of the withdrawal to the best of his ability to understand such information. While "I will take you for a walk at 4:30 tomorrow afternoon." will never come to mean to your dog exactly what you intend, you can train expressions like "Not now!," "Not yet!," "Soon!," and "Later!" as effective conveyors of timeframe expectation given consistent use, sufficient repetition, and dependable follow-through.

As this chapter closes, observe that frequent or sustained *Withdraw!* commands are very frustrating to one whom you have taken as a dependent and one who looks to you for satisfaction of his needs. Develop ways in which you can satisfy those needs according to your schedule, and you won't need to use the command so often. However, when you must, deliver the *Withdraw!* gently, but relentlessly. After all, it is a command.

The *See!* Command

Often articulated as "Listen!" or "Observe!" the *See!* command tops our list in its efficacy for introducing new skills. *See!* directs your student to "Watch this and learn from it!"

In your professional life, you use the *See!* command in virtually every training situation. You issue it when you ask a subordinate to read some information or ask one worker to observe how another performs a task. You also issue it whenever you call attention to any situation or activity, intentionally or not.

An effective *See!* command is made possible by a social bond in which both leader and follower share an appreciation of mutually interesting information. All intelligent creatures alert each other to things of common interest and, with most species, those higher in the social order typically provide useful information to the rest of the pack. Indeed, in many societies, an expectation of one's ability to provide useful information goes hand in hand with one's position in that society.

As an owner, manager, or trainer, you should occupy a position in your pack sufficiently exalted to sanction your use of *See!* commands (so long as you have something to announce that is interesting or useful in the opinion of your student).

The desired response to a *See!* command is a quiet, alert state that optimizes gaining your student's focused attention. As the first step, you must get his output activity to subside, because it is not possible for him to attain an alert, receptive state while communicating in an output mode. Moreover, halting output activity usually creates an observing state of mind automatically.

In order to get your student into a quiet alert state, use a quick priming sequence of *Look!*, *Stop!*, and *Wait!* commands. Once he is in a quiet, receptive state, the next task is to motivate his interest in your target by instilling an expectation that he will see something of personal interest and value by observing what you target. This is not always an easy task, especially in the beginning, for several reasons.

The biggest challenge with the *See!* command is that it requires substantial deference to the trainer by the student. The *See!* command requires that your student target and observe a source of information that he would probably not observe if left to his own inclinations. While achieving a state of alert observation is natural for any intelligent creature when driven by his own interests, mastering the *See!* command requires you to learn how to aim your student's attention according to your intention.

For an example of the difficulty this command may pose, consider high school students attending their daily math class. Most will easily follow the instructions that get them into the classroom and positioned in their seats. They have no problem "seeing" who is there and what everyone is wearing, eating, and playing with, or any of a full gamut of competitors for high school students' enormous powers of observation. However, getting their mouths quiet, eyes focused, and minds tuned to receive the mathematics instruction that the lecturer is hoping to provide can be a huge challenge. Clearly, the intentional *See!* command works most easily on those inclined to be ideal "students" in the strict sense of the word, that is, motivated, intelligent creatures that are actively seeking training with high interest and drive to learn.

In the workplace, topics of personal interest that motivate compliance with *See!* commands include financial reward, intellectual stimulation, or other satisfactions that come with an improved ability to do the job. With high school math students, often the predominant incentive is the fear that they will need to show mastery of the subject on tests or risk failing the class. Although it would be better to create an expectation that what they will learn by following your *See!* commands will interest or otherwise benefit them, sometimes a trainer must start by settling for less lofty motivation to get the process going.

With your dog, the difficulty with teaching the *See!* command is greatly exacerbated by his relatively low intelligence and markedly different natural interests. In order to overcome such challenges, you must instill an expectation that paying attention to anything you target for him to observe will be good for him in some way. The easiest way to do this is by making it a frequent practice to command him to *See!* things that interest him before and more often than telling him to *See!* the things that just interest you. Start with the easiest targets, that is, the things he would most want to observe even without your direction. Point out things like squirrels or birds in the back yard. Hide small treats under tables or chairs or in a remote corner when your dog is not observing you and then, at a separate time later, call his attention to the treat by pointing at the area and saying, "See your treat!" thereby offering an instant reward when he investigates what you tell him to observe. Another technique is to call his attention to various toys as you present them to him by name with excitement, as in "See your ball!" or "See your chew bone!" This reinforces his learning of the command, while you also use it to introduce names for his toys. Continuing in this way on a frequent basis, you will establish an appreciation of shared observations with your dog. Moreover, his frequent enjoyment of observing the things you tell him to *See!* will make you seem even more useful to him; that is, it will further empower your ability to lead him.

There are as many uses for the *See!* command as there are things to teach. It is the ideal command to introduce conceptual associations such as sounds or cues with objects, positions, or actions. The technique is as simple as introducing the object while at the same time saying the name in a way that sustains his observation of the association. For example, saying the word "sit" while coaxing him to take and maintain the position helps him to learn the association of the word with the position.

Drill the *See!* using exciting activities such as pointing out your observation of intruders in your shared space. When you hear someone approaching, say something like "Who's that?" while showing an intense, quiet interest. An additional benefit of obtaining a quietly focused inquisitive behavior in this situation is that it also discourages barking. Even a dog knows he cannot bark and listen at the same time.

It is instructive to observe how just leaning toward a targeted location while appearing to listen intently will cause a similar behavior in your dog, at least until you establish a history of faking it too often. The technique works well with people too. Just try standing on a busy corner while staring and pointing at the roof of a nearby building!

Develop the *See!* command to encourage your dog to share information with you by getting him to ask you to see things. If, as often will be the case, your dog hears and reacts to an intruder first, just say, "Who's that?" and listen intently while quietly praising your dog for alerting you. If you know who it is (perhaps another family member), say the name to share that interesting information with your dog. By your acknowledgment, you encourage his natural tendency to alert you about the intruder's presence by creating intentional rapport-building moments of mutually shared quiet observation of a third party.

Of all our commands so far, it is most important to use patience when teaching the *See!* command. Unlike other commands in which you may have an option of employing sheer physical force to gain compliance, complying with the *See!* command requires willing mental cooperation; you cannot force it. Sell the upside to him for observing what you target and minimize reprimanding him if he fails to do so.

While you may reprimand sustained nonquiet behavior (failure to *Stop!*), there is no good reason to reprimand your student for not observing what you have targeted with your *See!* command. After all, it is your role as the trainer to present your target in such a way that it does interest him. If you do this adequately, he will observe. If he does not observe, consider the possible reasons, tune your approach, and try again. As his receptiveness to observing the targets you suggest increases because of his frequent good experience when doing so, you will begin to realize the immense power of the *See!* as a training tool for both of you.

The *Show!* Command

Just as *See!* is the best command for introducing new concepts and skills, *Show!* is the ultimate command for eliciting performance. *Show!* is the command that directs subordinates to demonstrate what they know, want, or can do in response to an established cue. It is also the command to request ongoing adherence to established standards of behavior.

The cues used to issue a *Show!* command may be as varied as the behaviors one might want to command. The prerequisites to using the *Show!* are an established conceptual association of the cue signal with the requested behavior and a desire by the subordinate to please his commander.

The distinguishing hallmark of the *Show!* command is successful delegation of control by the commander to his subordinate to perform what has been commanded. In many ways, all the commands we have studied thus far could be considered *Show!* commands, in that each directs performance of some known behavior on cue. The better developed these other commands are, the more they become like *Show!* commands, as the student learns to demonstrate the requested behavior on his own without further coaxing or direction other than, perhaps, the command cue itself.

Early in its development, the intentional *Show!* command can be quite fragile. More than any other command, proper execution requires that you have first earned the trust of your student and have established a shared set of expectations about what is proper responsive behavior to your cue and what is not. Only with this foundation in place can you successfully delegate control to your subordinate to perform what you expect and to achieve the results that you desire.

When performed correctly, *Show!* is the most useful and enjoyable command for manager and student alike. Unless the requested action is uncomfortable, most intelligent creatures welcome opportunities to *Show!*

When an intelligent creature believes he can take the initiative to perform what is expected and thereby achieve a good result, he will naturally want to do so. Encourage your student to enjoy performing per your cue by consistently recognizing and rewarding him for doing whatever you direct him to do. Expecting that he will get something he wants by saying "Yes!" to your requests will motivate your student to learn all kinds of *Show!* commands.

An example of the *Show!* command from the workplace is when you command "Answer the phone!" to your receptionist. In such a command, you are saying, in effect, "Show me that you want continued enjoyment of our employment relationship by saying, "Yes," to my request in the manner you know you should, that is, by answering the phone in the polite way you know I want you to answer it!"

Another example is when you command "*Sit!*" to your dog. When you do this, you communicate, "Show me you want to please me and possibly get a good consequence by saying, "Yes," to my request and taking the sitting position that you have been taught as the proper response to this cue.

One kind of *Show!* commands are requests for information, which are usually worded something like "Show me!" or "Tell me what you know!" The proper response to such a command is that your subordinate shows you what he wants or tells you what he knows. As usual, this is easiest when he expects that something good will come to him for telling you.

In every case, the correct protocol is to give the command cue clearly and then to step back to allow your subordinate the opportunity to say, "Yes," to your command by displaying under his own control the behavior you have taught him.

Effective managers recognize the importance of stepping back and giving their subordinates room to perform what was requested (as agonizingly difficult as this can be at times). When managers consistently request subordinates to show what they can do in this manner, they encourage desirable behaviors throughout their organizations and, in particular, a deeper sense of personal responsibility. On the other hand, managers who issue *Show!* commands without shifting to an observing responsive style of behavior often stifle such development.

A common mistake of less-skilled managers is to ask a question and then answer it for the subordinate before he does. Another is to assign a task and then fail to let the subordinate carry it out with the level of independence that he expects. Such mistakes compromise the power of *Show!* commands, because most subordinates will not go into "showing" behavior and take the initiative to pursue requested actions unless they feel comfortable that their leader will accept and reward that which they show. As you have probably observed in your managerial life, allowing subordinates to show what they are capable of doing on their own also increases their satisfaction with you as their leader.

Just as is the case with your human subordinates, empowering this most important command requires an environment of trust. Your dog needs to trust that when he shows you according to the rules that you have taught him for the specific cue, he will be rewarded for his performance. Certainly, you cannot expect from your dog the same degree of initiative, intelligence, or self-management that you might from a human subordinate. However, with consistent encouragement, your dog can learn to perform many activities on command according to his ability and experience and how well you teach him.

A great but more advanced use for the *Show!* command to your dog is to teach him how to tell you what he wants. It is something you can do while communicating primarily in an observing mode. For example, when you observe your dog exhibiting behaviors that indicate a need to relieve himself, a good teaching technique is to use an anticipatory question, something like, "Do you need to go out?" As he goes through his repertoire of mannerisms attempting to answer "Yes!" to your anticipatory question, employ the reactive style by ignoring or rebuking any unacceptable signals and comply only with those responses you want to train as acceptable "Yes!" signals to your question. Catch him making his request in a good way, and then immediately reward him by complying with that appropriate request signal.

Another opportunity to teach your dog how to tell you things occurs around his eating activities. Eating is important to your dog, and he will display certain behaviors to let you know when he is hungry. Stimulate him by saying something like "Do you want to eat?" and then respond favorably to those attempts to say "Yes!" that are in accordance with how you want him to tell you so.

In the beginning, these techniques require that you observe closely and anticipate that he wants to tell you something even before he knows how to tell you. By asking him, you stimulate him to show some display of excitement and encouragement to you. If he responds by looking in a particular direction or by trying to lead you somewhere, get up and follow him. The more he expects that his proper signal will cause you to take action to satisfy his request, the more likely he is to provide the signals you want.

As your dog learns acceptable and effective ways for telling you things and achieves satisfaction from doing so, the experience will build his trust and enhance his overall happiness as he gains control over his environment. Instilling this ability broadens your usefulness to him as well and his willingness to defer to your leadership. After all, the ability to tell his leader what he wants in a way that will likely elicit a favorable response is something that every intelligent creature wants.

One important cautionary note is that, more so than with any other command, training the *Show!* is an ever-present process because your student interprets most reactions you make to his behavior as rewards or reprimands, regardless of whether your reaction was intentionally made. Your student's receptivity to such feedback makes unintentional training of potentially bad *Show!* commands especially easy to do. Simply responding to an undesirable behavior in a way your student perceives as favorable trains such bad behavior effectively.

Consider the act of feeding scraps to your dog at the dinner table in response to his begging. When you give those scraps, you teach him that showing begging behavior is a viable method for getting treats. Not only is occasionally giving into his begging bad owner behavior because of the dangers to your dog's digestive health, more importantly, it is bad for the health of your relationship because of the confusion you create by rewarding him on some occasions but scolding him at other times for what he sees as essentially the same behavior of begging at the table. Over time, through similar bad training, he will become less sure that he should show what you have taught him to show in general because he is less sure of what your reaction will be when he does so.

Stay keenly aware of when and what you are teaching as you respond to his behavioral initiatives. Make the *Show!* command strong by providing consistent consequences to his displays of behavior. Invoke *Show!* commands only with clear intention to provide good training.

(Of course, by all means, if you do enjoy having your dog beg for food at your dinner table, train him well to do so by always giving in. However, do not unintentionally train him that begging is a behavior that yields unpredictable yet highly polarized results. That would be unhealthy for your relationship.)

In the chapters ahead, we will look at many examples of using *See!* and *Show!* command combinations to train and elicit a wide assortment of behaviors. For now, recognize that the *Show!* is the empowerment command and that performing the *Show!* properly requires shared trust, a clear understanding of what is expected in response to your cue, and a critical emphasis on relinquishing control to your student to perform the things that you have taught him to do.

Part Two

SECTION TWO

Advanced Command Training

Make the Most of Your Command Skills

In the previous section, we introduced seven basic commands to serve as the foundation for all of the commands that we will study in this book. While we could have chosen a different command set as our foundation, the specific commands are not the most important thing. Commands are simply tools. Your vision and motivation when leading will always be more important than the tools you employ.

Our objective in this section about advanced command training is to make the most of our basic commands by using them to develop a broad portfolio of leadership tools, with many practical applications. Starting with a review of command training fundamentals, we will then consider our purposes for directing as well as how to tune our directives to fit the purpose intended by the command. Following that, we will consider specific techniques for developing additional commands and gentle directives to suit virtually any purpose that one might want. We will also look at ways to tune your directives to request activities more precisely. As you know from your managerial experience, the more precisely you can direct a broad spectrum of behaviors, the easier and more rewarding your leadership role becomes.

While a broad command portfolio is desirable, in order to be truly useful in a practical sense, commands must be reliable under even the most challenging circumstances. We will study techniques for increasing and maintaining reliability in a chapter especially about developing this crucial characteristic.

In the last chapter of this section, we consider a less obvious but nonetheless important benefit that can be learned through command training. This benefit comes from developing your ability to recognize "commands" issued to you by others. Such recognition can enable you to remain in charge when supposedly subordinate creatures seek to control you. The smarter your student, the more he will mimic your command techniques to get what he wants. You will want to make the most of this phenomenon to help you to understand your student better.

Focus on the Fundamentals

In any learning endeavor, whether it is in business, academics, or sports, what most obviously differentiates the advanced practitioners from the rank beginners is their facility for executing the fundamentals consistently. That is why most training programs intended to advance proficiency invest large amounts of time drilling on the fundamentals. With this in mind, we now begin our advanced command training section with the comfortably familiar activity of reviewing our fundamentals.

Like all training that we advocate in this book, we seek command training that is good, effective, and intentional. We achieve this kind of training by constantly focusing on three essential keys:

- Know what it is that you wish to train (and why).

- Have a consistent system of effective incentives in operation at all times.

- Observe and adapt continually to meet the requirements of the situation.

These are all things that you, the leader, must do. Your student's role in meeting these prerequisites is quite passive; he needs only the aptitude to learn what you are seeking to train. This important difference between the roles of trainer and student is especially apparent when training a dog.

The reasons for providing command training cover the same gamut of reasons for training anything. Command training improves compatibility by providing a means for you to elicit behaviors that you find compatible and to discourage those that you do not. Command training allows you to increase the utility that your subordinate can provide, as he learns and wants to perform per your command the useful things that you have taught him to do. Command training educates you and your student about control mechanisms important in any leader-follower relationship. Last, but certainly not least, command training provides opportunities for your pleasure and that of your student, as you each learn new ways to influence the other to get what you each want.

In order to attain reliable command compliance, your subordinate must truly want and choose to comply with your commands. His value system must say to him that obedience to your commands is the best thing for him. You instill such a value system through consistent use of incentives and acknowledgements.

An expectation that you are a benevolent provider of what he needs motivates deference to your leadership. As you train commands, never compromise your student's expectation of your benevolence, even when he falls short of your obedience expectations. You want him to obey you mainly because he knows that it pleases you, which is also good for him, and not only because he fears reprimand.

Positive communication stressing opportunity for reward provides your student with a compelling incentive to comply with your commands, while his firm expectation of rigorous enforcement helps to discourage disobedience. Associate this powerful pair of contrasting consequences with every command you issue. With time, like any conceptual association, repeated experience will make the association stronger and hence more influencing of his decision to comply when you issue commands.

The most crucial aspect of your behavior when doing command training is consistency. The only way to get your student to 100 percent compliance with your commands is for you to be 100 percent consistent when delivering commands and command-related performance consequences. Every opportunity counts; any reward that was expected but not given is perceived as a reprimand, and a missed expected reprimand is perceived as a "got-away-with-it" reward. Avoid confusing expectations of consequences. Be consistent when acknowledging your student's performance of your commands.

Our Fundamental Rule of Training, "Tune your training approach and content according to your objectives and your student's needs," applies to command training just as much as it does to any training. As you strive to build and strengthen your command repertoire, consider your purposes in issuing each command and what benefits from your student's perspective that his obedience to your command could gain him.

When you give commands, observe your student's responses carefully. Intentionally hone your reactions to his responses to tune his performance. Continually evaluate whether your responses actually causes the change you were seeking. In particular, did your response help make what you were commanding clearer to him? Did it cause him to try harder to obey? If not, try something else. Observe your student intently and learn what works for him. Then, make that work for you. After all, as his trainer, you are the one who has to motivate him to do what you want him to do!

Always consider the big picture when giving direction. While relentless enforcement of compliance with the direction you suggest may be appropriate when needed, not very many purposes really warrant it. Directives that have been issued as commands always warrant strict enforcement, because the very essence of a command is that you always enforce it. On the other hand, most unimportant directives that you may choose to give do not warrant relentless enforcement. Issuing unimportant directives in the form of commands is counterproductive simply because there are limits to the amount of control to which any autonomous intelligent creature will submit. In order to direct everyday behaviors effectively, strive to avoid using commands when they are not needed. Rather, strive to employ gentler requests when possible. Obtaining voluntary conformance with your gentle suggestions is a far better indicator of your leadership success than forced obedience to your strict commands.

Before we start to create new commands, I will offer a few additional reminders related to command training. New commands skills are easiest to teach in a classroom environment suitable for the kind of command you wish to teach. Always be clear about your intention when conducting formal command training. Start each training session by announcing that you are doing so. Make the word "training" one he loves to hear and anticipates eagerly.

When conducting formal command training sessions, put heavy emphasis on using *Look!* and *See!* commands, coupled with intense observation and immediate feedback on your student's every action. Encourage any progress you observe, and never reprimand a failure beyond simply refusing to reward it. Always signal the completion of your formal training sessions with praise and acknowledgment rewards for his participation. Your student's enjoyment of the learning process will have a lot to do with how eagerly he will try to learn.

Direct with a Purpose

Any good, effective, and intentional leadership directive that you may wish to give should start by contemplating your purpose for issuing it. The purposes for issuing directives fall into one or more of the same four categories as the purposes we studied for any kind of training:

- compatibility

- utility

- education

- pleasure

In this chapter, we examine techniques for delivering directives within each of these purposes by employing our basic commands as commands or, more often, as gentler forms of giving direction. The purpose you intend to achieve by your directive is crucial to choosing your approach and to choosing whether you should deliver your directive in the form of a formal command or as something lighter. As we will see, more often than not, the light touch is the right touch.

Directing to Enhance Compatibility

The primary goal of most early training or orientation exercises is to encourage compatibility. As you seek to develop compatibility, you must first determine exactly what conforming behaviors you require to enable peaceful coexistence. Obtaining conformance is much more important with some things than with others. Strive to accommodate your student's preferences when you can, because the more that you require him to conform instead to your preferences, the more he must change and so, the harder both you and your student must work to change him.

The first five of our basic commands—*Look!, Stop!, Wait!, Come!,* and *Withdraw!*—are all useful for building compatibility. The following are some examples of using these commands and directives of a softer variety to enhance compatibility:

To Build Rapport

When you want to encourage compatibility by building rapport, *Look!* is your first and foremost appeal. The *Look!* rarely needs to be issued or enforced as a formal command. Use it gently and frequently as a welcome invitation to greet and bond. For best effect, associate *Look!* with acknowledgment rewards on a frequent basis.

To Discourage Incompatible Behaviors

For the sake of compatibility, most people need to protect their own sense of order and control by setting boundaries on the behaviors of those around them. (Actually, dogs do as well!)

Consider thoroughly your reasons for any behavioral boundary that you intend to impose on your student. As much as you can, plan your intended reactions to observed violations of your boundaries in advance. Develop a mental portfolio of graduated responses that you will use to enforce the boundaries that you set. Having such a plan before it is needed will go a long ways toward enabling you to deliver intentional, measured, and consistent reprimands when observed violations do occur. Furthermore, while doing this exercise, if you realize that you are unable to develop an effective scenario for enforcing a contemplated boundary, you can use that insight to avoid the folly of demanding a boundary that you cannot enforce. In either case, such thoughtful preparation will encourage respect for any boundaries that you set.

When seeking to discourage incompatible activities, *Stop!* is the ultimate "incompatibility command." In fact, one of the best indications of the level of incompatibility is how often one employs forceful *Stop!*

commands. When you need an immediate, unwavering cessation of an activity, use the *Stop!* command as forcefully as required. However, if you wish to become more compatible with your student, strive to use *Stop!* less frequently and be as gentle as you can when you must use it.

Substitute a *Look!* for the *Stop!* command in anticipation of incompatible activities. *Look!* tells your subordinate, "I am aware of you and observing your actions." A gentle reminder that he is under observation usually encourages a subordinate to avoid reprehensible behavior, because he expects an immediate reprimand otherwise. In the context of contemplated bad behavior, *Look!* is the more friendly way to coax his decision to conform with your expectations than is the more confrontational *Stop!* command.

Another downside of using *Stop!* to quell incompatible behaviors is that besides carrying the overhead of a confrontation, this command also begs follow-on suggestions of alternative behaviors to sustain it. While you might first define unacceptable behavior by using a *Never do that!* form of the *Stop!* command, the goal is to have your student's avoidance of unacceptable behavior become self-directed and self-sustained. For this reason, using a strong *Withdraw!* is a much better way to direct sustained avoidance of incompatible behaviors. It says to your student, "You can exhibit almost any other behavior you like and remain in good favor, but you cannot do that one!"

To enable this gentler approach, your student must recognize an abundance of acceptable behavior options from which he can choose. Rather than needing to push your student away, pull him by the reward of increased autonomy to choose from many enjoyable options available to him and the hope of receiving positive acknowledgment for his compliance with your restriction.

To Obtain Time to Resolve Issues

As the command to sustain the status quo, *Wait!* may be an obvious choice of directives to buy time when needed, although it is not necessarily the best. We will observe in the next chapter how to use time-specific directives such as *Soon!* and *Later!* delivered more like a *Withdraw!* to establish a timeframe for resolving a subordinate's request for your attention while freeing him to pursue other activities of his choosing while you do so. This approach promotes compatibility by lowering his feeling of the need for immediate satisfaction until a better time for you.

To Request a *"Chill Out!"*

When you are engaged in any high intensity exchange that you wish to discontinue or diminish, especially if you were the instigator or enabler (for example, when you want to get your dog to stop the roughhousing that you started and that has now gotten out of hand), *Withdraw!* is a far better command than *Stop!* because it is less confrontational. Avoid promoting a situation that might require confrontational enforcement to cool down when a gentle *Withdraw!* command is easier to deliver and obey. Just say something like "Cool it!" while you disengage and look away. Another good alternative is first to distract by requesting some form of a *Show!* command like a quick "Sit!" or "Show me what you want!" in order to recognize and acknowledge your follower briefly before disengaging. When trying to calm things down, keep cool and avoid appearing confrontational.

To Obtain Compliance with Your Leadership Directives

When you require compliance with your leadership as a prerequisite for compatibility, you can request a wide variety of compatibility-enhancing behaviors using *Come!* command training techniques. Make it a frequent practice to look for, acknowledge, and reward compliant behavior, even when you are not actively requesting it. As you know from your human management experience, defining the behavior that you want and then proactively rewarding the good citizenship that compliance represents is far more effective than spewing out endless streams of reactively reprimanding *Stop!* and *Wait!* commands.

To Establish Physical Boundaries

You can extend the well-trained *Withdraw!* command by applying it to situations or locations other than those immediately proximate to your person. When your purpose is to set a physical boundary, first employ

See! commands to identify the boundary and then use variations of *Withdraw!* commands to sustain them.

With your dog, *Withdraw!* is an excellent supplemental tool for territorial control, such as when declaring rooms of your house off-limits. Properly delivered and understood, it says to your dog that he can go to any of his allowed places in good grace, so long as he stays away from the forbidden spaces. The proper training technique is to announce a restricted area as he approaches its boundary by using a *Stop!* sustained for several seconds with a *Wait!* while using understandable words or gestures to define the boundary, followed by a *Withdraw!* to suggest he go elsewhere.

To illustrate, when I want to define a room as off-limits to my dog, I have him sit at the boundary while I move my hand back and forth across its doorway in a wigwag kind of motion to define a threshold that he is not allowed to cross without explicit permission. After much practice using that signal in the context of many doorways, my dog and I have learned to use this signal effectively with almost any doorway anywhere. The key is always to use that same signal and never to let him cross the boundary once the signal has been given. Respect for physical boundaries is easy to train; all it takes is a clear definition of your boundary, consistent enforcement (including forcing him to leave restricted areas immediately when he ventures into them), and frequent rewards acknowledging his respect for the established boundaries when he stays in the places he is allowed to visit.

To Establish Behavioral Boundaries

One behavioral compatibility boundary most owners want their dogs to understand is that they must not impose on people who are eating at the table. To instill this, you must teach that he will never gain anything good by approaching people in dining situations and that he risks an unpleasant reprimand for doing so. Use the *Withdraw!* command technique of avoiding eye contact or other engagement, punctuated when necessary by a sharp reprimand (a brief but very intense *Stop!*) for his persistence, followed again by immediate and complete withdrawal posture. If you do it right, your student will prefer withdrawing to receiving a confrontational reprimand. Your dog must know that he can go sit in a corner, curl up in his bed, or do many other things; he just cannot ever approach or attempt to engage you until after you leave the dinner table. You should not have to be mean about it, but you do have to be very strict.

Consistently sustained reinforcement behavior that he associates with his approach to your boundaries will teach your dog to avoid crossing them. As he learns what your boundaries are and that it is best for him to respect them, your need to issue boundary reinforcement commands explicitly will subside, save the occasional yet very necessary reminder every time he forgets.

(This same technique of sustained nonacknowledgment will also work to quell uninvited interruptions or invasions of your space at work. It just takes consistency and a willingness to appear a bit impolite while training this behavior to your subordinates.)

Directing to Achieve Utility

Once an acceptable level of compatibility has been achieved, another important purpose for giving directives is to elicit behaviors through which you can derive the usefulness that you had in mind when you took on your student.

The commands *Stop!*, *Wait!*, and *Withdraw!*, while needed for compatibility-enhancing behaviors, are of little help toward eliciting greater utility. Certainly, the *Look!* remains useful for opening channels and promoting clear communication. However, the *See!* and the *Show!* are the power commands when it comes to training and directing useful activity.

While *See!* may well be the command most favored by trainers, *Show!* is always the command preferred by skilled managers. Trainers use *See!* to create a conceptual association of the meaning of a directive with its cue. On the other hand, the *Show!* command provides the actual means to reinforce learning and to obtain the benefits that motivated the training.

We will explore using the *See!* for education and other forms of training in just a moment. First, we consider how to use the *Show!* command to get students and subordinates to perform upon request activities they already know and can do. The better we are at eliciting the performance of known behaviors on cue, the more value we can achieve from our investment in training.

To Request Information or Solicit Input

Asking for information or soliciting input are highly useful applications of the *Show!* command. As you should know from your management experience, obtaining information from those you lead can enhance the quality of your leadership decisions immensely.

My dog and I have happily advanced the *Show!* command to serve as a means by which he can be quite specific in telling me what he wants. Whenever my dog attempts to engage my attention, I direct, "Show me what you want!" This causes him to sit close for petting if that is what he wants, head for the front door (he prefers to pee in our front yard: a territorial marking thing to be sure), head for the back door (to his designated pooping area in our back yard), head for the kitchen (his feeding area), and so forth.

Sometimes I use forms of the *Show!* command to suggest things to my dog on which he has some choice, such as, "Show me if you want to go on a walk!" which encourages him to display a level of excitement based on his real interest level. At forks in the road on unfamiliar off-leash walking paths, I often say, "Show me which way!" which lets him enjoy being the lead explorer for a moment while I amuse myself watching him anxiously ponder such weighty decisions on his own. I find especially entertaining the times when he has to improvise showing behavior to teach me about something new that he wants. I try to make it a point to observe and respond in the way I think he would want me to respond to what he shows me. As do subordinates in the workplace, your dog will try much harder to provide information to you when he believes that you will put that information to beneficial (as he perceives it) use.

To Request Performance of Known Activities

The *Show!* request is the way to lead a subordinate to demonstrate anything that he knows how to do. In your day job, virtually every directive that you issue in the execution of your managerial duties is done as some form of *Show!* Variants used commonly with dogs include requests to display a position or activity such as *Sit!*, *Lay down!*, or *Shake!* As these cues and their associated behaviors become understood, you can grow your use of *Show!* command techniques to request almost any activity or behavior.

Rather than making your student respond to your pushing him to perform, let the allure of a potential reward pull him to decide to perform. Any student, including your dog, will learn to want to respond per your direction if you convey that you expect him to perform, if you give him the space to do so, and if he expects that you will reward him for his successful performance. Provide the signal, stand back in expectation of his appropriate response, and let him perform. After he has performed per your request, provide good consequences as appropriate. This simple technique will work to elicit the performance of virtually any behavior that your subordinate already can do.

Directing to Achieve Education

Education comes from learning conceptual associations, usually through repeated observation. Commands for educating include *Look!*, *Come!*, *See!*, and *Show!* As usual, *Look!* is essential to encourage clear communications channels. *Come!* encourages the submission and cooperation needed to draw your student's attention to your agenda. Introduce conceptual associations using *See!* techniques and reinforce them using *Show!* techniques to reward him for demonstrating that the association has been learned.

To Instill Any Conceptual Association

See! is the command for instilling any conceptual associations. Simply get your student to observe consistent, repeated simultaneous manifestations of two or more things you want him to associate, and his brain will take over from there. Consider his level of intelligence and avoid associating too many new things at a time, because that could muddle his perception of crucial relationships like cause and effect.

To Teach the Meanings of Words

Word meanings, which are simply associations of a sound or visual cue with a concept, can be easily taught using *See!* command techniques. Name your dog's toys by presenting each toy to him while saying its name and repeating it often in many contexts. "Here is your ball!" "Is that your ball?" "Give me your ball!" "Do you want your ball?" or "Where is your ball?" All these expressions associate the word "ball" with the object in a way that makes him think about it in multiple contexts.

Strengthen words like "good" by repeating them whenever good things are happening. Say them often when your student is doing something he enjoys doing, like eating his dinner or receiving a reward.

Use tones in your delivery of words like "Bad!" and "No!" to clarify your meaning. Develop an assortment of "no" sounds using a common reprimanding tone to create a set of incentive reprimands ranging from instant gentle "Ack!" sounds and stop words to progressively stronger deliveries. I use a warning word, "Inappropriate," spoken syllable by syllable in a very slow, deliberate, and intense voice to provide a sustained incentive reprimand that holds his attention and gives him a little time to hear and contemplate my warning.

"Bad!" said using the same reprimanding tone in a strong voice is the strongest in my series. I use that word only as an acknowledgment reprimand and not as an incentive reprimand. While "Not good!" may be a nicer way of saying the same thing with people, dogs are less likely to recognize the meaning of the modifier "not" and thus may become confused by hearing a favorite word being used in such a negative tone and context. Reserve a unique and strongly delivered word like "Bad!" for giving acknowledgment reprimands, and develop a series of softer ones for to use for incentives to prevent reaching that point.

While it requires significant intelligence to generalize the meanings of words widely, even your dog's understanding of a word can be strengthened by associating the word with multiple situations in which the word has relevance. Words like "up" and "down" can be generalized by associating them in multiple contexts like going up or down stairs or up or down hills on a walk or in commanding body positions.

To Introduce New Commands

Command cues requesting a specific behavior require first building an association between the cue and the behavior. Use *See!* command techniques to establish a receptive state of mind that facilitates instilling conceptual associations. Patient repetition with timely consequences, especially with earned rewards, is the key to associating new command cues with the desired actions or behaviors. We will study how to associate cues and expected behaviors to create and teach new commands in the following chapter, but first a word about achieving the purpose of achieving pleasure as you train.

Directing to Achieve Pleasure

As much as possible, every directive you give should include a purpose of achieving pleasure for you and for your subordinate. One pleasure you can expect comes from getting ready compliance with your directives. The pleasure that your subordinate gets comes from his associating compliance with an improved sense of well-being and comfort with your leadership.

While there may be little reason for you ever to issue directives that you do not expect to result in something you want, realize that there is little reason for your dog to obey commands from you that do not offer him an opportunity for achieving the pleasure of getting something he wants. Keep a purpose of shared pleasure as a motivator whenever directing your student, and you will get much better results.

Develop Your Command Repertoire

In this chapter, we will study how to develop a broad repertoire of command cues using adaptations, extensions, and hybrids of our original seven basic commands.

My approach to this subject of developing your repertoire is intended to offer you the widest range of options to develop useful commands per the choices of application that you should make, according to your personal preferences. Rather than attempting the impossible task of addressing every possible command, I will present just a few examples of how you can build upon our seven basic commands by adapting them to new yet similar purposes. As you progress in your understanding, I encourage you to use your imagination to identify additional purposes for which you may want to develop custom commands and then to apply the material presented here toward doing so. This subject matter of developing new commands and command skills is best learned by doing.

Developing useful new commands can be quite simple. Start by identifying an appropriate behavioral objective. By appropriate, I mean a behavior that is within the physical and mental capabilities of your student and a behavior that you want and will reward. Be very certain to understand your purpose for your new command before you attempt to teach it, because more than anything else, your purpose should guide your approach to teaching it.

Name the target behavior you desire and identify the cue that you will use to request it. Consider how your new command is similar to commands already learned and apply what you have learned through teaching previous commands to guide you in selecting the cues and the techniques that you should use for teaching the new one.

Break complex tasks into smaller ones and teach them in increments that your student can handle. You and your student need to establish a history of incremental "wins" to encourage continued mutual interest in learning new things.

As usual, should you encounter challenges to your training efforts, remember that you are the one who must adjust your methods to get what you want. You should not expect such a high level of adaptability from any student or subordinate (and, most certainly, not from your dog).

The following examples illustrate the application of my approach to developing new commands along with effective techniques to train them:

The "*Drop!*" Command

A useful variant of the conditional *Stop!* is the *Drop!* command. *Drop!* should be taught in the same manner as *Stop!* including, when needed, physical enforcement. Your human management experience offers many familiar examples such as "Drop the argument!," "Drop the project!," or "Drop the bad client!"

Drop! says, "Let go of that which you are holding!" It is a command to release something; it is not a demand to hand it over to you or anyone else. If, as may occur early in training, you need to force compliance with your command with a physical take-away, then you should drop the item as soon as you take it away. Do not hold onto it or imply it was taken away by you. Attention should be focused on compliance with the command, not competition for the object.

Much like the *Stop!* command, *Drop!* is often unwelcome, may need substantial enforcement, and, if issued without offering a suggestion of alternative behavior, leaves little hope of being sustained. Also, like the *Stop!* command, *Drop!* must be enforced in a way that is decisive, that avoids prolonged conflict, and that rewards compliance immediately. Reward compliance with your *Drop!* command by praising your student and, if appropriate, by offering him something else to hold, ideally something even more engaging. With a project manager, that might be a new project to manage; with a salesperson, that might be some new prospects to replace a dropped unproductive account. With your dog, giving him a treat or a toy to hold or even engaging him in an entirely new activity will work best to sustain compliance.

The "*Off!*" Command

Off! is useful for directing a dog to depart his immediate location or to desist from his pursuit of another object. *Off!* is an extension of the *Stop!* with nuances of the *Withdraw!* command. Use it to command your dog to exit a neighbor's lawn before he does any damage as well for preventing your dog from pursuing items of interest that may not be good for him, such as another animal or spoiled food.

Like the *Stop!* command, with sufficient practice in a broad context, the meaning of *Off!* should become clear in any context. As with the *Stop!*, always deliver *Off!* firmly enough to gain immediate compliance. Support your command using as much reinforcement as needed to achieve the result quickly and thereby minimize any perception of prolonged conflict. As with the *Withdraw!* command, *Off!* should also offer your dog the reward of having many other acceptable options, so long as the forbidden object is avoided. Promote these other options. As with any restrictive command, it is far easier to get your dog to pursue alternative attractions than it is to sustain his avoidance of the one he has currently chosen to pursue.

Variants of the "*Wait!*" Command

In certain situations, you may want to convey a notion of time or other expectation that is more specific than what the basic *Wait!* command conveys. You can add many nuances as you grow the vocabulary that you share with your student. For example, "Wait here until I get back" commands a subordinate to sustain position, while "I need some time to think about it" contains elements of a *Wait!* as well as of a *Withdraw!* as it releases him to pursue other things while you consider the issue. *Stay!* tells your dog to hold position while he waits, whereas *Later!* is more like a *Withdraw!*

Giving a specific time or condition for ending the wait is informative and encouraging for those who can understand such information. With humans, we often issue *Wait!* commands that entail complex conditions such as "until after you become eighteen" or "when you successfully complete your training program," or "until four o'clock on Tuesday afternoon." With dogs, such complex conditions are more difficult to communicate.

Simple concepts such as "Wait for my signal before taking your treat!" are easy to teach to a dog. Just present the treat by setting it down a few feet from him, command him to *Wait!* and never let him get his treat until you give your "Okay" signal. Begin by making the duration of his wait something he can sustain on his own, even if only for a few seconds, and then build on each previous success by stretching it out for longer periods.

Almost as important as learning that he will certainly be reprimanded and thwarted in his unauthorized attempt if he goes for his treat before you signal "Okay," your subordinate must also expect that upon reaching the specified time or condition, you will indeed lift the restriction and address his issue. Such expectation comes from experience; nothing will weaken this expectation more than failing to lift the *Wait!* when the expected conditions have been met.

Not yet! is a different kind of hybrid directive that you can train to acknowledge your subordinate's anticipation for you to lift a *Wait!* that you imposed. *Not yet!* reiterates the need to continue waiting while confirming that the *Wait!* will end, albeit without specifying when. While perhaps not as satisfying as precise detail about when the wait will end, *Not yet!* is sometimes the best one can do, especially with dogs. Responding with a calm but firm *Not yet!* is always better than just ignoring your subordinate's expressed sense of urgency, regardless of species. It tells him that you recognize and are aware of his desire and that you will deal with it at some time in the future that you, not he, will determine.

Soon! is another expression to provide encouragement that a reward for showing sustained patience is imminent. As with any cue, your student's interpretation of the meaning of *Soon!* will be learned through his actual experience. To get the best effect, only use *Soon!* when you anticipate that the wait will end in a timeframe that the subordinate considers adequately near-term. The perceived meaning of *Soon!* depends very much on the context; it may be three months for a job promotion or three minutes for dinner. Be certain that both you and your subordinate share that context.

The *"Get with the Program!"* Command

A common extension of the *Come!* command, *"Get with the program!"* demands your subordinate to accept and submit to your agenda. Another popular variant is *"Do what you are supposed to do!"*

"Get with the program!" presupposes that "the program" has indeed been formulated and communicated, which further assumes that you know what your program is. When you give a command as challenging as *Come!* or any of its extensions, it is imperative that your subordinate understands the expectation of your command. The best way to communicate your program is by using *See!* command techniques to introduce its elements and *Show!* command techniques for reinforcement. Be unswerving in staying on-message about your program.

Train *Get with the program!* exactly the same way that you train *Come!* Seek out and recognize conforming behavior and encourage it as being good because it is "with the program." Catch it happening, acknowledge it, and reward it. Use polarized consequences to teach your subordinate to expect that doing what he is supposed to do is always the best thing for him. Reward his demonstrations of adherence to your program generously, especially in difficult situations. Also, always be clear that not getting with your program when commanded to do so will never be tolerated.

As with the *Come!* command, you must never issue a command to *"Get with the program!"* in a situation that is not important enough to warrant relentless enforcement. A command is never an optional suggestion. For less important things, use softer suggestive requests that encourage voluntary compliance with your agenda. Your goal is to create a relationship that allows a light touch on your part while encouraging your subordinate to offer faithful compliance willingly with your program.

The *Take!*, *Fetch!*, and *Find!* Commands

Take!, *Fetch!*, and *Find!* are popular commands that you likely employ often in your human management role (albeit, hopefully, with politely humanized wording and delivery). When possible, just as you would with human subordinates, give these "commands" to your dog as polite requests unless circumstances make instant compliance important. Training these commands to a dog is quite straightforward once we understand what each new command entails in the context of our basic commands.

Take!, *Fetch!*, and *Find!* are hybrid *Show!* commands that contain elements of both the *See!* and *Come!* commands, in that they require identifying an external target and approaching and submitting. Train these new commands to your dog with enthusiasm in a series of small steps using conformance approaches. Start by using *See!* commands to identify and name the target item that you will want your dog to take, fetch, or find. Let him see, smell, and taste the named target item by placing it gently in his mouth as you say, "*Take!*" Praise him for accepting and holding onto it, even with your gentle help, and then ask him softly to drop it, followed by more praise. Next, simply point at the item, say, "*Take!*" while naming the object (as in "Take the ball!" or "Take your toy bone!"), and give him even more praise when he does so. You may have to do this quite a few times over several training sessions before he understands that you are asking him to pick up your targeted item on cue. Reinforce associations of your command cues with performance of the requested activity through frequent practice and praise.

Fetch! is an extension of the *Take!* command in which the target object is either already some distance away or is thrown farther away by you. Invoke it by pointing at the named target object, saying, "*Fetch!*" while pointing to and encouraging his approach to the object. As he completes his approach, say, "*Take!*" to get him to pick it up, "*Come!*" to follow you to your original spot, and then "*Drop!*" to release the object. Follow each full cycle immediately with a lavish reward. Repeat often but never to a point of inducing boredom with the interaction. After your dog comes to expect the *Fetch!* command will always be followed by the other commands, you will no longer need to use them, as your dog comes to associate the single command *Fetch!* with the entire sequence of expected actions.

Find! is a more challenging command in that requires memory of the object by name and where it may be in addition to a search, a fetch, and a return to you. I like to issue *Find!* by starting with a *Look!* followed by a questioning tone like, "Lance! Where is your ball?" to get him thinking before I issue the command, "Go find your ball!" I usually make him find it on his own, even if it takes him a while. On the other hand, if he has thoroughly exhausted his search, I do help him find the object by finding it myself and then helping him "see" it by pointing and calling out the object's name. This is also a great opportunity to strengthen the *See!* by using it to help him find something important to him that he truly wants to see.

To make our *Find!* command more broadly applicable, I like to practice requiring my dog to find a variety of differently named articles. Sometimes, he will cheat and bring the first one he finds instead of the one I specified, in his attempt to satisfy my request quickly. I don't reprimand him for cheating like this, nor do I ever let him get away with it; I simply restate my request with a little more emphasis on naming the target clearly. I think my consistency in this matter has helped my dog become more discerning of my requests in general while still enthusiastic to be commanded to find his toys by name. Ultimately the *Take!, Fetch!,* and *Find!* commands are all great opportunities for your student to perform per your request and thereby obtain rewards. They are not unlike *Sell!* commands you might give to your salesforce. They offer your dog more ways to get what he wants from you by simply doing what you ask him to do. That should be quite pleasurable for both of you.

The *Sit!* Command

Positioning commands and other calls to perform an action are all variants of the basic *Show!* command. In order to train the *Sit!* command to your dog, start with a *Look!* (just say his name or catch his eye) to open the communications channel. Next say, "*Sit!*" in a commanding tone and demonstrate by touching just above your dog's tail area with a very gentle downward pressure to provide a physical *See!* command that helps him learn what the command cue intends.

Should your dog resist mild pressure on his tail area to sit down, do not try to force the *Sit!* in a way that meets continued physical resistance. That would communicate competition; the *See!* command demands cooperation. Step away, disengage, and then re-engage with another *Look!* command by calling his name intently yet encouragingly, followed by again saying, "*Sit!*" with a repeated gentle indication of the desired position and patient expectation.

If this technique still does not work for him, try changing your technique. An alternative way to indicate the sitting position is by raising your dog's chin gently, which often causes a dog to back off into a sitting position in response. A third alternative is to step in toward him so closely that he backs off by sitting.

With a little adaptive maneuvering, one way or another, you will eventually get him into the sitting position. As soon as he demonstrates the position, reinforce it with praise to confirm the association of the request cue with the position. The next step is to teach him to expect that if he attains the position per the established cue without additional coaxing, then you will reward him. Once he knows what the command means, remember to give him the space to decide to sit on cue rather than maneuvering him into it. Soon, that cue will suffice without additional coaxing, as he takes control of achieving the sitting position himself.

Delays in compliance encountered during early training of new commands often indicate a weakness in association of the cue with the desired behavior. Remedy this by tuning your approach to instilling that association. Usually it just requires additional patient presentations of the cue and the expected result together, but sometimes it may take a change from your initial approach. Experiment with many different ways of making the association you wish to make using friendly *See!* command techniques to learn what will work best for your dog.

The technique just discussed for teaching the *Sit!* will work for requesting any position that you wish your dog to attain on your command. Once your student understands the meaning of the command cue, simply train compliance using *Show!* command reinforcement techniques. The proper routine to drill any variant of the *Show!* is to command, expect, and reward. The goal is to get your student to perform per your directives under his own control because he chooses to do so, not because you force him to do it.

After you give a command, if you are certain that your cue has been understood, punctuate it with your silent anticipation of his appropriate response. Allow him a respectful amount of time before attempting to reinforce your cue with additional nurturing. Quietly expect him to assume the position you requested, give him space and time to do so, and then reward him when he finally does perform. If he fails to perform, just start over with a *Look!* command, followed by your cue for the position that you want shown. Support his compliance with your directive with your best and most patient "encouraging him to show" behavior.

The more variants of the *Show!* command that you teach by expecting him to listen to your cue and choose to follow it, the more you will be able to teach him.

The *Down!*, *Side!*, and *Rollover!* Commands

Certainly, in your human management capacity, you know it is best to train in layers, basing each more complex behavior on well-known simpler behaviors. The same concepts apply when training your dog. Train complex behaviors in layers. Build each new increment on the foundation that comes from successful execution of simpler *Show!* commands.

A fun example of a more complex *Show!* command for use with your dog (and one that is typically too complicated to teach directly) is the *Rollover!* command. (Caution: A "rollover" may not be a comfortable move for some dogs, especially older or larger ones, so, as a matter of respect, please don't persist in training the *Rollover!* if your pet shows physical discomfort with the move. The steps leading up to it, however, are easy enough for any dog to learn and perform.)

Rollover! should be taught in a series of steps. First train the much simpler *Sit!* command. Once *Sit!* is reliable, introduce *Down!* by attaining the *Sit!* position and then coaxing your dog to move his front paws forward until he is lying down and then praise him and repeat the cue word for reinforcement. Drill the *Down!* command as a distinct command cue by recognizing and rewarding him while he is in the position. Next, advance the command to be performed upon a single command from either a sitting or standing position by commanding, expecting, and rewarding compliance. This may take days or weeks to become reliable, depending on your dog and your skills as a trainer. Practice often in short sessions, offering meaningful rewards.

After the *Sit!* and *Down!* commands become reliable, train the *Side!* command by first getting your dog to lie down. Then command "*Side!*" while coaxing the position of lying on his side. (Belly petting with verbal praise works well for this.) Repeatedly reinforce association of the cue word, the position, and reward. Next, train your dog to achieve and sustain the *Side!* directly from any initial position. Always reward him while he is still sustaining the requested position, not after he leaves it.

After *Side!* is well learned, if you choose, you can refine your *Side!* command by specifying which side you want down. I teach these commands as "*Side—Down Side Left!*" and "*Side—Down Side Right!*" as refinements to the previously learned *Side!* command by praising him only when he lays on the designated side and, when he lays on the wrong side, withholding any reward while gently encouraging him to change sides until he does so. When he gets to the requested side, I reinforce the association by restating the name of the side down while he is lying on it and rewarding him.

After building the foundation of using simpler commands to position for a rollover, issue the new *Rollover!* command as a suggestion to your dog while he is in the side position and initiate the rollover by gently helping your dog roll over to his other side. Then immediately praise and reward him. Do be careful that your dog recognizes you are in training mode so he is less resistant to or surprised by your attempts to help him roll over. You want to avoid feelings of alarm, competition, or conflict when training. Keep it fun by being positive and encouraging of all his attempts to please you.

****

Time spent training and drilling not only serves to instill specific new commands; it enhances overall trainability. With enough repetition, your student will learn to expect a pattern of command cue recognition, responsive action, and reward as a common routine in his formal training exercises. You will be able to train commands that are more complex because his experience of being rewarded for successfully learning simpler commands motivates his desire to be your student. Also, just as importantly, with thoughtful practice, you will become better at issuing commands in a way that he will happily receive and obey them.

Obviously, there are nearly limitless options for creating very specific commands. In every case, the proper method is to identify your purpose, define and communicate the specific cue and expected result, and then seek out and reward success. While this may take a lot of ingenuity and patient encouragement on your part, especially when training complex commands, such patience is appropriate to your role as the trainer and fosters a relationship that promotes a mutual enjoyment of training.

I will close this chapter by sharing a personal anecdote of my experience with training one of my dogs, a Labrador mix named Lance, that you may find amusing, if not illuminating.

Lance had come to enjoy command training sessions and was very receptive to being taught and commanded to perform tricks. When I intended to conduct a formal training sessions, I began by commanding him, "Lance, show me that you want training!" which he did by running to the designated training area (my living room) and sitting attentively while he waited for me to go load up on treats and come back to issue my next command. After requesting a *Look!* to signal that class is now in session, I usually started with a few simple commands like *Down!* or *Crawl!* to warm up. This reinforced a positive training environment by providing quick and easy opportunities for success. Like most people, most dogs love success, even when performing the simplest of challenges.

If Lance anticipated that I was intending to drill a new command that he had recently learned, he would sometimes ignore responding to my warm-up commands and without waiting for any command cue, immediately perform the new trick he anticipated that I would request. I know I should refrain from rewarding this lack of attention to my specific command, but I sometimes lacked the self-discipline to withhold his reward from him, thereby encouraging his "Let's get to the point" shortcuts. It constituted unintentional training to be sure and is very probably something upon which I need to improve, but any dog's intention to please me just to get a reward as quickly as possible can be amusingly disarming.

(In my life as a manager, I wonder how often I encouraged human subordinates to take questionable shortcuts because I was enamored of their attempts to get their assignments done quickly. Unintentional training of errant showing behavior can be so easy to do in almost any situation.)

On the other hand, I have also observed that occasionally yielding permission to show me whatever acceptable behavior he wants to show me makes me appear more useful to my students and subordinates. I believe that by occasionally allowing my dog to take the lead in showing me what he wants to show me, I increase his pleasure with our association. I enjoy it too.

Yielding control is a fine option that does not compromise your leadership in any way. You simply must remain in charge of the decisions to delegate control and when to take it back. As you must already know from your successful management experience, effective leadership does not require controlling everything. The same is true when guiding your dog's behavior. Encourage him to show you things he wants to show you. He will enjoy the opportunity, and you may learn something from it. It may even lead to you observing new behaviors that he already knows and that you can learn to command of him by giving the behavior a name and associating a cue with it. By issuing the cue whenever you observe the behavior and rewarding it, you will create the associations necessary to elicit the behavior on your new command.

Strengthen Reliability

Reliability is a vital attribute that you will want to make part of every command that you employ, because any unreliable commands can diminish the strength of your commands across your entire portfolio.

Achieving reliable compliance requires that your subordinate readily recognizes your command cue, that he understands how to perform the behavior it specifies, and that he willingly chooses to comply.

Recognizing commands cues comes with the familiarity fortified by practice. With your dog, help him recognize when you are issuing a command by consistently using a characteristic commanding tone of voice and a firm but calm demeanor. Consistent delivery instills deep conceptual associations that enable your directives to be recognized instantly as formal commands by the tone alone.

When issuing a command cue that is already well known to your subordinate, a direct communication style is appropriate, because well-trained commands should not need further exposition or embellishment. Encourage compliance with a reinforcing style to hone precision. Reward exactly those behaviors that you want and ignore those that merely come close. While reprimanding "merely close" behaviors could send confusing signals, by rewarding only the exact behavior, you narrow the behaviors associated with an expectation of reward and thereby refine the meaning of the command without discouraging his attempts to please you. Precise commands must usually be taught in stages and continually honed with drills focused on mastering the details of refinement at each stage.

By far, the most effective way to strengthen any directive that you may choose to give is to increase your subordinate's inclination to accept you as his leader. Almost any subordinate will find gently delivered commands more comfortable to follow, especially *Look!, Come!,* and *See!* commands. After all, what intelligent creature would choose to open communications with, much less approach, an angry maniac screaming, "Come here right now, you stupid dog!" at the top of his voice? Command cues are most compelling when delivered in a strong, quiet, and respectful way.

The strongest of all commands are those that do not require any cue to effect because they are already understood and anticipated. Do not expect this level all the time; after all, your subordinate is unlikely to be clairvoyant. In any event, you can help him toward this level of self-sufficiency by continually reinforcing his knowledge of what you expect of him by consistently recognizing and rewarding his good decisions, especially those he makes of his own volition.

In the remainder of this chapter, we will review and offer techniques for making each of our seven basic commands more reliable. You can extrapolate these techniques to any variations or derivatives of these basic commands in your repertoire by using the same techniques. We start with our easiest command, the *Look!* command.

Strengthening the *Look!* Command

Strengthen the *Look!* by using it frequently in a positive context. Develop your calling of his name into something that your subordinate likes to hear. Too often, some managers fall into a bad habit of reaching out for subordinates only when they have something to demand or criticize. Avoid this kind of ineffective behavior with your dog. Make it a good habit to say hello in a friendly way as often as possible. Keep receptivity solid by using *Look!* for more than just priming subsequent commands that you want to issue. Use it on its own to build rapport.

Strengthening the *Stop!* Command

A strong *Stop!* is instant and complete, even under difficult circumstances. Its domain, that is, the assortment of activities that the command will actually cause to be halted, also speaks to the strength of the *Stop!* command that you share with your student.

One way to strengthen the *Stop!* command is by providing greater specificity about what to stop when issuing it. Target the behavior you want stopped as precisely as you can to avoid implying a request to stop anything more than what you want stopped. This will make your *Stop!* commands more palatable to obey.

Except as a regular compliance-training drill offering quick rewards, avoid overusing the hard *Stop!* for minor things, and never command your subordinate to stop something over which he has no control; his likely failure will only frustrate and weaken the command. In day-to-day interaction, try to use milder, less demanding interruptions. Your ultimate goal is to achieve a level of compatibility such that forceful use of *Stop!* is rarely indicated. Suggest other desirable alternatives as your customary approach to interrupting the activities you choose.

A *Stop!* that is anticipated is more likely to be a strong *Stop!* command. With conditional stops, teach your student when self-imposed stops are appropriate by always imposing the command as a gentle reminder in such situations, like when approaching an intersection on a walk. As your dog becomes more familiar with your expectations, you can use milder cues such as a raised eyebrow or a mild "Harrumph!" to suggest that he stops.

Make the *Never do that!* more reliable by always confronting every display of disallowed behavior with a reprimand of sufficient impact to discourage recurrence. The fact that he expects to get an immediate unpleasant rebuke whenever he misbehaves makes the need for actually issuing *Stop!* much less frequent. While it may be a challenge for the leader to maintain such vigilance and instantly reactive behavior, intense focus during early training pays off well in the long run. However, any lack of certainty that his unacceptable behavior will be interrupted is effectively an incentive reward, offering him a chance at getting away with it. The target level of reliability requires that your student knows what constitutes unacceptable behavior and prefers to avoid it. The only way to train this is by confronting unacceptable behavior whenever you observe it so that it leaves no doubt you will always confront it.

I offer one more suggestion about strengthening the *Stop!* command with a training exercise that is good for reducing aggressive behavior in dogs around protecting food. Such tendencies can be dangerous for guests or children who might inadvertently interrupt the dog while he is eating. I recommend you develop this ability with your dog at an appropriate point in his and your relationship. It illustrates how, using positive reinforcement, you can easily obtain obedience even in very difficult *Stop!* situations while you also develop desirable behavioral traits as a side effect. The simple technique presented here may be extrapolated to many situations.

After (and only after) your dog has learned to trust that you always take care of his need for food, at some time while he is actively eating his meal, call his name and then follow with a firm but gentle *Stop!* command. Be prepared to intervene physically, like gently stepping between your dog and his food bowl to ensure compliance, because eating is one activity that he probably does not want to stop. Do not amplify or even repeat the command; he heard you the first time. Just force him to stop calmly, firmly, and relentlessly; do not let it become a struggle. As soon as he does stop, have him sit and wait briefly. Reward him immediately with an even better tasting food treat than his usual meal, augment that reward with lavish praise, and then immediately direct him to return to his meal. With repeated occasional practice (over days and weeks but not often repeated during a single meal nor at every meal, which might become very annoying), he will come to recognize that the interruptions that occur when he is eating are really potential opportunities to get extra special rewards more than bothersome interruptions or threats to getting his nourishment.

Important note: For this training exercise to work, you must first develop the essential prerequisites of trust, command cue recognition, enforcement expectation, and his overall perception that your commands usually present opportunities to be rewarded for compliance. Without these, this recommended training exercise could go quite badly.

When you can cause immediate and consistent obedience to your *Stop!* command in such demanding situations, you are well on your way to developing the command to the power needed.

Strengthening the *Wait!* Command

The ability to suspend activity in the face of distraction for an extended duration is the mark of a strong *Wait!* command. Encourage your student to conform by letting him know that you recognize and are pleased by the fact that he is patiently waiting. When possible, remove any doubt about when the waiting period will end. Your subordinate's compliance depends on his expectation that his waiting period will eventually end with a reward for him having waited. The implication that waiting will result in a good thing makes waiting an acceptable choice; doubt that anything good will come because of waiting discourages his motivation to comply.

As with the *Stop!* command, the most useful *Wait!* is not one explicitly issued by you, but rather, one that is anticipated and willingly entered into by your subordinate. This anticipation is enabled by your subordinate's expectation that you routinely address his desires within a reasonable timeframe, so he is okay with waiting and will even initiate doing so on his own.

In human situations, you know that you should keep your subordinate informed about when his next assignment, break, paycheck, performance evaluation, or salary review is to occur. Similarly, your pet should have set expectations of when he will be fed, let out for relief, walked, or engaged in training or playful activity. Expectation of a schedule for your attention to his needs also lessens the likelihood that your dependent will interrupt you with a demand for which you will have to issue a *Wait!* or *Withdraw!*

We previously discussed how to strengthen the *Wait!* by extending duration and increasing distractions, first independently and then combined. Another technique to make the *Wait!* reliable is to drill it for shorter periods. Issuing shorter *Wait!* requests allows you to give more frequent and immediate rewards for embracing your request to wait and entering into the expected behavioral state. As your student's experience increases his with his compliance being quickly rewarded, he will become more receptive to complying with the *Wait!* command as a good command to follow. In order to strengthen both receptivity and sustainability, intersperse the technique of quickly issuing and rewarding many short waits with that of issuing occasional long and distracted *Wait!* commands that you should reward even more emphatically.

While making employees wait for their paychecks in a workplace situation may have legal ramifications, we have more latitude related to our rights with our dogs. I often command my dog to sit and wait for his dinner, from a few seconds to almost a minute, to keep him happily reminded that complying with my *Wait!* always ends well. Sometimes, if he has compliantly waited for an unusually long time or in spite of my leaving the room, I put an extra treat in his bowl on top of his regular dinner right before I release him from his wait. Because he expects a reward for his patience, he no longer seems to mind even long waits. Over time, continually reinforcing his expectations has created for him a value system that encourages his willing compliance. He knows it is the right thing for him to do!

Strengthening the *Come!* Command

As the command to approach and submit, *Come!* and its variants are among the most important commands available to managers or trainers. Strengthen these kinds of commands through frequent drill in a positive context. Consistently contrast the rewards and encouragement for conformance with quick and firm challenges to any observed nonconformance. Instill the expectation that conforming to your beck is the only viable option, while you simultaneously promote his perception that obedience to your beck is an easy and potentially rewarding choice.

As discussed when we introduced the *Come!* command, one of the best techniques for strengthening such commands for submission is to issue them explicitly whenever you observe your student already engaged in the activity of his own volition. Simply catch his behavior and associate it with the command cue and with good consequences by rewarding it.

Good managers will often enforce getting with the program by demanding the performance of some very specific activity. For example, demanding and recognizing on-time arrival at work is a small thing, but it does associate easily achieved good results for compliance with the program. Gaining compliance with even just one aspect of your program is at least a step toward achieving compliance with most or all of it. Take it one step at a time to achieve eventual conformance with your entire program. If you cannot get conformance with some one aspect of your agenda, consider de-emphasizing that item from your program at least temporarily, if it is not that important.

When training your dog, should he ever resist a *Come!* command, immediately go to him (walk to him; don't chase him, which would suggest competition) and physically bring him to the spot from which you requested his approach. Scold him while he resists or avoids, but praise him as soon as he does submit to being in the requested location. After he submits, any continued scolding of his initial resistance is counterproductive; a big reason he eventually complied was to avoid more scolding. He will comply more quickly if expects the scolding will stop instantly and turn to praise as soon as he shows his decision to change his behavior. Turning up the contrast of the likely consequences at the point of decision is quite effective in eliciting good choices.

Never accept dawdling noncompliance in response to *Come!* commands. His failure to comply immediately with any command that you give and that he recognizes indicates one of two problems. The first is as an unacceptable challenge to your role as the leader, which is typically called insubordination. The second possible problem, and one you should consider before assuming the first, is an indication that your command was poorly timed or issued, in which case you should rescind the command and rethink your objectives. Never try to force compliance with your inappropriately issued directives, because that will eventually weaken your ability to command just about anything reliably.

Strengthening the *Withdraw!* Command

Strengthening the *Withdraw!* does not mean additional avoidance of you by your subordinate; it means training him to know when not to impose upon you. As one of the more permissive commands, *Withdraw!* yields control over his activity to him so long as he avoids approaching the forbidden space while the command is in effect.

The mature *Withdraw!* is best delivered firmly, and when possible, it should minimize any implication of reprimand. At its best, the *Withdraw!* is a friendly request to stay away for a while. Normally, this will be acceptable to your subordinate, assuming that he has other good options. The best technique to strengthen the command is to learn softer and subtler ways to issue it. Hand signals, headshakes, eye-frowns, or similar nonconfrontational body language lessen the potential that your subordinate will interpret the *Withdraw!* as a reprimand. Both people and dogs alike prefer rewarding gentle commands with their willing compliance as opposed to rewarding undesirable reprimands with their forced compliance. Otherwise, they are simply training their leaders that strong reprimands are an effective way of dealing with them. Smart subordinates know better than to do that!

Withdraw! commands, when consistently delivered in a particular situation, instill a conceptual association of that situation with a desire for avoidance. Sufficient repetition trains self-imposed compliance with your specified restrictions. If you ever reward an undesired approach with pleasant attention after issuing a *Withdraw!* command, you will foster an expectation that it is sometimes okay to approach in that situation. This will teach your student to engage in endless experiments trying to distinguish when it is okay to ignore your command. This phenomenon is ubiquitous, whether with your subordinates at work, your children, or your dog. Be gentle but consistent and unwavering with your *Withdraw!* commands.

One final recommendation for developing a reliable *Withdraw!* command is to avoid overusing it. Overuse of the *Withdraw!* can be quite destructive to a relationship because it discourages rapport. If you observe a tendency on your part to use *Withdraw!* too frequently, think about why.

If you are using *Withdraw!* too much because you feel he approaches too often or is too needy, consider the reasons for his persistent approaching behavior as well as the reasons for your perception of it being excessive. It is unusual for any intelligent creature to continue to approach someone who never provides benefits, especially when given other options. If he continues his attempts to engage you in spite of your reprimands for breaching your restrictions, it may be because he perceives that you are not sufficiently available to satisfy his needs, or he may not have enough alternative places he can go or things he can do. Another possibility is that you may be doing something that encourages his excessive dependency on you. Regardless of the cause for any of these situations, you are the one who needs to figure out the cause and modify your behavior to correct such problems.

Strengthening the *See!* Command

Your goals in strengthening the *See!* are to widen the spectrum of targets that your student will observe on command and to improve the speed and depth of his compliance. Since the *See!* is so difficult to enforce directly, having your student want to follow this command is of utmost importance. Such desire comes from his expectation of reward for focusing his attention on the target you select.

Any student is naturally inclined to observe certain things just because they interest him. Develop his inclination to comply with your *See!* by frequently suggesting shared observation of things that he would naturally choose to observe with or without you. Anticipate and tell him to *See!* what you target whenever you become aware of something that you think will interest him. Name the things you want him to observe, and use those names as part of your *See!* commands.

Whether your student is human or canine, the techniques to strengthen the *See!* are quite similar. Identify the target, stimulate interest in it, indicate what you want observed as precisely as possible for your student, and promote that seeing what you want seen will enable him to get rewards. Positive experiences resulting from actually obeying the *See!* reinforce receptivity to it. Through many positive experiences, you will generalize and strengthen the reliability of *See!* as a powerful teaching command.

Strengthening the *Show!* Command

A reliable *Show!* command enables you to get behaviors that you want from your student, both as default behaviors and in response to your command cues or even more subtle directives.

Ideally, you have selected your student in accordance with what you intend to train him to be, because an aptitude to be trained in the behavior is an absolute prerequisite to an ability to perform it. No matter how great your technique may be, you will never teach your dog to read your newspaper aloud to you. You must observe and respect limitations in the ability of your student. A good trainer always respects the difference between stretching such boundaries in a positive developmental way and breaking the student's foundation of comfort and self-confidence by insisting he master challenges beyond his reach.

Respect your student's learning limitations, and strengthen each *Show!* command based on your providing a record of rewarded incremental successes. Through repeated successful experience with easier variations of *Show!* requests, your student will better learn how to be trained to perform new and more challenging command cues and behaviors. Nothing encourages future success like past success.

As your training progresses, you will first recognize your student is gaining mastery of your *Show!* commands when he begins to anticipate and make good decisions on his own: ones that are congruous with your expectations. You are gaining true mastery when you begin to let him make those decisions on his own. The most reinforcing reward that you can give for showing well is to give even more *Show!* command opportunities and, in particular, ones that let your student take even greater initiative and control over how he shows you what you want of him.

The greatest benefit of all that comes from strengthening the *Show!* command is in the creation and reinforcement of desired default behaviors. Observe your student carefully to catch behaviors as soon as they are manifested so you can intentionally provide timely consequences to encourage the ones you want.

As with all commands, reliable performance of *Show!* commands depend on both the student's natural ability and his desire. Given that there is little you can do about his natural abilities, your best option for strengthening your commands will always be to focus on increasing his desire to obey.

Listen for Requests

In this final chapter about getting the most from command training, we examine the special phenomena of your student learning and mirroring your methods in an attempt to exert control over you. The more intelligent your subordinate is, the more likely he will attempt to manage you in the ways that you manage him. However, to be the real leader, you must remain in control by consciously choosing how you react to the signals and cues he uses to make his requests of you.

Responding compliantly to directives from subordinates in an unconscious or unintentional manner is an abdication of your leadership position; the prerogative to direct belongs only to the leader. On the other hand, responding positively with intention and purpose to his requests increases your subordinate's perception of your value to him and empowers you even more to lead him.

There are three keys for you to get the most from your subordinate's penchant for making requests of you. The first is to be aware of his requesting behavior—when and why he is doing it. This awareness comes from thoughtful observation. Second, always acknowledge his request so long as he makes it in a way that you find acceptable. Letting him know each time that you hear and understand his properly made request will train him to make his requests in a way that will elicit your most appropriate response. The third key is to choose your response intentionally. When you obey his requests without consciously deciding to do so, it really does raise the question of who is leading whom.

Let's use the framework of our seven basic commands to examine some examples of requests that your subordinate is likely to make of you and the appropriate responsive behaviors that you should employ:

Look!

Humans and canines alike often issue the *Look!* without regard to rank, although one's relative role does determine whether one may issue it as a command or only as a request. In order to build rapport, learn not only how to give the command; learn also how to receive, acknowledge, and when appropriate, even reward your subordinate's *Look!* request with one of your own.

As an experienced manager, you already know just how important it is to recognize when others are requesting your attention. As a caretaker, you should always acknowledge any *Look!* from a dependent as long as it was delivered appropriately. Encourage his appropriate attempts at communication by listening closely to his message. If you choose to decline his imbedded request, then do so separately but do not reject his attempt to open a channel. Acknowledge polite attempts positively, demonstrate that you understand his imbedded request, and then respond to his request as a separate matter based on its merit.

An inappropriately issued *Look!* (for example, one done too forcefully, perhaps by barking loudly or jumping up in your face) should be rebuffed just as you would rebuff any rude interruption. Discourage such inappropriate attempts to dominate you by responding with *Stop!* or *Withdraw!* commands. As the owner, manager, or trainer, it is your prerogative to define how your subordinate should politely initiate communication.

How you respond to subordinates who ask you to *Look!* speaks volumes about your personal management style. I have always preferred working for managers who encouraged me to initiate and engage them in communication. I suspect that most dogs prefer caretakers who respond well to their requests for attention. Train your student to seek your attention in the way you prefer, and you will be more likely to respond appropriately when he does.

Stop!

It is natural that your student or subordinate may attempt occasionally to issue a *Stop!* to you. Because of your relative roles, it is only a request and not a valid command. Nevertheless, I recommend that you reflect on why your subordinate issued the *Stop!*, and unless you have a greater purpose for persisting (one that is within the prerogative of your role), you should honor his request to stop. Why wouldn't you?

Wait!

When a subordinate issues a *Wait!* request, it is either an act of gross insubordination or a reasonable request for time—one that you would do well to acknowledge and accommodate. Carefully evaluate which it is before you react. Your subordinate probably would not have requested a *Wait!* were he not feeling some level of distress already. Few good leadership objectives are ever accomplished by increasing levels of distress.

Another type of requesting behavior associated with the *Wait!* command is what I call the Anticipatory *Wait!* wherein subordinates accustomed to getting rewards for waiting behavior will occasionally self-initiate waiting behavior in hopes of getting a reward. A workplace example of such an anticipatory wait is a subordinate sitting outside your office without an appointment, hoping to catch a few minutes of your attention. Other examples include your dog sitting by the door with his leash in his mouth, hoping for a walk or sitting at his dinner bowl to suggest that he is available for feeding.

Do not treat anticipatory waits as simply cute submissive obedience. They are actually attempts by your subordinate to direct you. If the waiting behaviors your subordinate displays are those that you want to train for making such requests, then encourage them by providing the requested reward as soon as possible after you observe the request. On the other hand, quickly dismiss any anticipatory wait for which you do not intend to provide the expected reward. Depending on the situation, this can be done with a gently rebuffing *No!* to indicate you don't intend to provide what he wants or a *Later!* or a *Not now!* or a *Soon!* to indicate that you will address his request at another time and that there is no reason to sustain his overt waiting behavior.

Waits are a suspension of activity in hope of reward. Keep the *Wait!* command effective as a behavior that you direct and do reward.

Do not dull the power of your *Wait!* commands by allowing sustained anticipatory waits that you do not intend to reward.

One more point on anticipatory waits: While you may want to discourage anticipatory waits by your subordinates, the self-imposed anticipatory wait is a useful behavior for you to exhibit when you are expecting response to a command that you have issued. Your anticipatory wait quietly sustains your issued command cue while encouraging compliance with it. The main difference is that, as the leader, you have the right to command.

Come!

It is certainly never within your subordinate's prerogative to issue any kind of *Approach and Submit!* command to you. It is quite unusual to observe a dog attempt such a request, unless trained (for example, when a guide dog is leading his dependent). On the other hand, in human interactions, I have often seen the *Come!* directive used effectively by subordinates to control their bosses without any apparent recognition by the boss of what is happening. This role reversal can be quite amusing, annoying, or both to observe in others around the office but, as the boss, you never want to let it happen to you without recognizing it.

However, relationships in which *Come!* requests are routinely issued by a subordinate and *consciously* complied with by the leader usually indicate that the relationship has risen beyond the command level. This can be a very good thing, as we will discuss in the next section.

Withdraw!

In a work environment, it is common for a subordinate to ask a manager to withdraw and give him some space. Similarly, our dogs occasionally need us to give them a little space and time of their own. They usually direct such a withdrawal by either walking away or by being nonresponsive to overtures. As with the *Stop!*, I can think of little reason to ignore a properly issued request to withdraw, as long as you establish a suitable time and place for eventual interaction according to your prerogative. Showing such respect to any subordinate who needs a little space is a vital component of good leadership.

See!

Ideally, an upwardly directed *See!* is an attempt by the requestor to provide information he believes to be of value to the leader. Sincere attempts are a sure sign of a good relationship; it is a most desirable form of rapport.

However, *See!* may also be used by a subordinate in an attempt to control his manager. Although this phenomenon is far more prevalent with humans, I have often observed my dog calling my attention to his treat box in an obvious attempt to direct me to give him a treat. He employs a classic *See!* and *Show!* sequence of requests to direct my behavior to his purpose. I am comfortable it is not an inappropriate role reversal so long as I remain consciously in charge of deciding whether to give him the treat. I would like to think that, for the most part, I do control the decision. My dog probably just thinks that I need more training to become consistently compliant.

Show!

Virtually any attempt by your dog or subordinate to cause you to perform a hoped-for behavior represents a form of a *Show!* request. Essentially, he is asking you to demonstrate a behavior that he wants and believes you know how to do. His request cue to you will typically be some action that he has associated as causing you to react in the certain way he wants you to react. Your consistent cooperation by following his request strengthens your subordinate's inclination to issue the cue in that way and to expect your performance. When you observe a *Show!* request from your follower, use it as an opportunity to train how you prefer to be asked to do the action he is requesting. And, of course, in order to stay in your leadership role, be sure your response is always a conscious decision.

****

In all cases, your student's directive behavior toward you is a natural and healthy manifestation of his intelligence. By responding intentionally according to your choice, you can provide very useful training to him about how to communicate with you properly about his needs and preferences. That enables you to move your shared relationship to a higher level. On the other hand, if your subordinate constantly controls you in a directive manner, you might want to consider the possibility that he may be clearer about his agenda than you are about yours. If that bothers you, then you are the one who needs to change. After all, he is just doing what you taught him to do.

Part Two

SECTION THREE

Beyond Commands: The Conversational Level

Why Commands Are Not Enough

While some may have thought command training would constitute the entirety of our training curriculum, especially when given the simple context of training dogs, it does not. If you want to get the most from your relationship and your leadership role in it, command training is only the foundation for the complete training program that you and your follower should share.

To be sure, command training establishes a useful and necessary foundation. Command training, when done with a steady emphasis on rewarding learning and compliance, reinforces your follower's expectation that your leadership is a good thing. Command training instills a useful set of tools for directing and eliciting specific responses. However, by itself, command training is insufficient to provide everything that you need to lead in the way that most want to lead or to be led.

Few good leaders actually direct much of anything important just by barking out commands to their obedient puppies. As gratifying as it may be for a dog owner to put his willing pet through a full regimen of strictly obeyed commands, would any normal person really want to limit interaction with his pet (or with anyone else) to only this? I believe that most good managers would choose to avoid displaying such "drill sergeant" personality traits in their daily interactions.

Moreover, leading any subordinate who does only what he has been commanded to do is a terribly unpleasant and arduous chore, much like rolling a heavy cube uphill one turn at a time. Indeed, a stubborn dependency on constant direction may be arguably the most insidious form of insubordination known to managers. Ideal subordinates, including dogs, should learn the correct behaviors and require only minimal ongoing direction to keep them rolling on their own along the right path.

I believe most good leaders prefer relationships in which communication flows readily in both directions. Even when giving detailed specific directions, most good leaders would choose to avoid functioning like an overbearing master pushing buttons on a control panel. Control panels, when carelessly overused, inevitably enslave both the supposed master and his hapless victim. Most good managers want to make the right things happen without the burden of too much button pushing.

If your ultimate objective is to have your dog do what you want him to do without a need for constant corrections, then he must naturally want to do what you want him to do. You must move past the command level and focus on developing your student's motivation to do what you want him to do beyond the limited context of only performing in response to your command.

Introducing the Conversational Level

I now introduce what I call the "Conversational Level of Leadership" as a model for leading that is far more powerful than what can be achieved through commands alone. The approach employs the technique of continually communicating about your own agenda as well as the agenda of your subordinate in order to motivate your follower to self-directed behavior that is consistent with your expectations of him.

At the conversational level, the leader must convince his follower that the leader's agenda includes (and even complements) his follower's own agenda for getting what he wants from the leader. Success is achieved when the follower truly expects that his leader has his best interests at heart and so willingly adopts his leader's agenda as an important part of his own. The reward for both is that the pursuit of the resulting shared agenda becomes self-motivated and easily directed.

An example of leadership at the conversational level in the workplace that I would hope is familiar to every experienced manager is an excellent working relationship with an ideal trusted subordinate. In such a relationship, you typically maintain open communications channels and readily exchange information. You readily beckon him to approach you and interact through comfortable conversations. You rarely feel it necessary to reprimand him. You can provide direction and even suggest different approaches with little conflict. You often ask him to do things, and you trust he will do them well without further direction. You rarely demand that he stop something, because he seldom does things that you do not want him to do. You rarely need to make him wait, because you trust his self-direction. You do not often need to ask him to withdraw, because he knows where and when he should approach. Your ideal subordinate most likely became that way (or not) in large part because of you and how you selected, trained, and treated him.

Effective managers observe their subordinates constantly and use what they learn to help align the motivations of their subordinate with their own motivations. Effective managers of humans strive to lead using open two-way communications with the people who report to them. The better that a manager uses effective conversations to keep relationships well-tuned, the more engaged and motivated his subordinates become.

These same conversational techniques will work splendidly toward achieving a higher level of enjoyment with your dog while alleviating many limitations of the command level. The main challenge for you will be learning how your dog's thinking works and understanding his motivations. This understanding is fundamental to providing well-targeted consequences to tune the behaviors that he exhibits.

As we pursue taking your leadership skill to this next level, I caution you to remain proficient with command techniques because they are required foundation for the conversational level. On the other hand, even if you have not yet developed a large repertoire of commands or fully mastered all of the commands or techniques that you would like to master, please do keep reading. Looking ahead to where you want to get by focusing on your ultimate training objectives should provide incentive and insight on how to get there.

The Art of the Conversational Walk

A great example of leading at the conversational level is proper on-leash walking that is enjoyable for both a dog and his owner. In contrast to jerking a dog about by a chain on his neck, as unskilled owners often try to "lead" their pets, conversational "on-leash walking" is the elevated art of moving along together with almost no tugging by either caretaker or dog. Movement is smooth and easily directed, even anticipated by both, because a gentle conversation about the walk is always in progress.

Teaching (and learning) this comfortable way of walking together is a matter of conducting ongoing "conversations." Start with a short loose leash attached to a harness suitable to control your dog (not his regular tag collar) and begin walking at a pace comfortable for both of you. The instant that any tugging whatsoever occurs, calmly stand still, issue a verbal *Stop!* command, and hold the leash firmly. Remain immobile; do not tug. Then issue a *Wait!* and observe closely for his compliance. Loosen tension on his leash the instant he voluntarily complies with your request. This will teach him that he is in control of the tugging of the leash and that if he walks compatibly, it does not tug. By leading him in this steady, gentle, but firm way, you stress cooperation rather than competition for control.

As you refine your walking routine through practice, use it as an opportunity to develop a broader vocabulary of directives like *Hold up!, Wait!,* or *Cross!* (which I use to signal my dog to cross a street with attention and alacrity). I regularly associate words like "left," "right," "up," and "down" with the direction on the path I am leading. Through frequent nurturing of these associations, we have developed a shared vocabulary of useful directives for leading my dog reliably, even when he is off leash.

Cultivate the meanings of directives like *Gentle!* by introducing such words in situations where your student is inclined to display gentle behavior naturally, such as when you are gently petting him. Encourage him with your praise and other rewards for his compliance. As he builds the association of the cue with the behavior, begin using *Gentle!* on your walks whenever you encounter other creatures to reinforce your expectation of socially acceptable behavior and then praise him for conforming to your request. With practice, calm reminders will evoke the gentle behavior, because it is an easy way for him to get something he wants. After enough good encounters, *Gentle!* will become a regular part of his behavior whenever he meets others on his walks, whether you remind him or not.

For you both to enjoy your walk together, your dog must be given some say about checking out the attractions he finds along the way. Observe and try to anticipate what he finds attractive so you can make your decision about whether to let him check something out in advance of him requesting to do so.

When you do choose to let your dog inspect something that he has politely requested to check out or when you see things you think he is likely to enjoy investigating, signal your approval clearly. Use it as a chance to strengthen your *See!* command by walking briskly toward the attraction while offering him a looser leash as your way of telling him that you know what he wants and are helping him to get it. Give words of encouragement and praise to add to his enjoyment of checking out the attraction that you helped him reach.

If you choose not to allow him to check something out, signal your decision by shortening up on the leash before he tugs on it, if possible. Do this very gently to train him in the polite language of the walking conversation. I use a technique of lightly vibrating one finger against his leash as a notice to him that, while I recognize he is interested, I intend to walk by the upcoming attraction without pausing. With consistent practice and enforcement, your dog will quickly learn what the signal means and comply.

Never allow your dog to lunge successfully, that is, to enjoy the privilege of checking out any target that he has just pursued by lunging.

Should he lunge forcefully, hold back firmly on his leash without jerking, command him to stop, and then command him sit down long enough to let his urge to control you dissipate (and maybe even long enough to annoy him a little for his misdeed). Then, after he remains calm, resume your walk, bypassing the attraction briskly. Be consistent and enforce this "no lunging" rule fully whenever necessary, and he will learn.

If he lunged at something that you would have let him check out had he asked more politely, then, on a subsequent walk, if he is behaving well, you may choose to direct his attention to that previous attraction and help him get to it. This will help him to learn that you really do understand his agenda and that you are useful in assisting him to achieve his agenda.

Whenever you take a walk together, make it an opportunity to hone your listening skills and those of your dog. The more conversational it gets, the better you each listen and the gentler your indications to each other can become. Through many ongoing conversations in which you reinforce your agenda for the walk while you acknowledge and accommodate his agenda along the way, you both will get what you want from your walks. Build the right expectations and keep them strong.

Foundations of the Conversational Level

Reflecting on the example of conversational on-leash walking, we next observe several important prerequisites to establishing a mutually enjoyable walking relationship at the conversational level. These same qualities are necessary as a foundation for any kind of conversational leadership:

- There must be something good for everyone in the conversation.

- Both leader and follower must know and accept their roles in the relationship.

- Effective communications channels must be in place and open at all times.

- The leader must be as willing to observe and adapt as he is to direct the behavior of his follower.

As the leader, you enable conversational leadership by creating a relationship with these qualities as its foundation. Let's consider the details of how this is done:

Ensure there is always something good for everyone.

Assuming you direct intentionally, most of your leadership initiatives likely meet the criteria of being good for you. Your job as his caretaker requires you to ensure your leadership is good for your dog as well.

In our conversational leash-walking example, the caretaker and dog each gets what he wants and expects from the walk. Through many positive experiences and interactions along shared walks, the caretaker-dog bond is strengthened. A most important caretaker role in our on-leash walking example is making sure that the dog gets to satisfy his agenda for the walk by being allowed to check out attractions, take care of business, and do other things he wants from his walk. Getting what he wants makes following his owner's agenda for controlling him less objectionable. As he learns that his conformance to the walking routine gets him more of what he wants, submitting to the leash will even become desirable.

Regardless of whom you may be leading, your roles as manager and trainer demand the cooperation of your follower. The Conversational Level of Leadership is all about maximizing the degree of that cooperation by developing a shared agenda and shared value systems.

The leader must learn from each student individually what constitutes effective consequences. While there may be many common motivators, such as food or affection, many nuances of these and other motivators vary greatly from student to student and even from time to time with the same student. The challenge for many managers to achieving conversational leadership lies in the enormous self-control required to focus on absorbing and acknowledging the agenda of another. The good news is that even a dog can teach his agenda to an observant trainer who wants to learn.

However, if you cannot comprehend or show that you understand what your student is trying to say to you, it will not seem like much of a conversation to the one you are trying to lead to a higher level of participation. Your follower will only participate when he feels the level of motivation that it is your job to provide to him. Such training requires (and your caretaker role warrants) that your program actually does offer him something that he wants or needs. Reflect on this often, and be sure it does. Be a good student of what motivates your follower.

Communicate and maintain your proper roles.

While I hope the role of each character in our dog-walking example was clear, I have observed on-leash walking in which the canine has become the actual leader while rendering his human to be his clueless follower. Although there may be appropriate intentionally delegated role-reversal situations, such as when employing search-and-rescue dogs, most of these cases that I observed were not the result of intentional good training but rather came from unintentional, bad, and yet very effective training caused by a failure of the leader to lead.

If you wish to maintain your leadership role, you must act the part. Do not mistake the conversational level as compromising any aspect of leadership authority. The prerogative to issue and enforce commands is clearly held by the leader and, most importantly, *only* by the leader. Working well together at the conversational level demands a mutual acceptance by both leader and follower of the very different roles that each plays in the relationship.

(Fortunately, considering this book's primary application, we benefit from the relative ease with which dogs and their owners typically accept their very different roles. As you may have observed, such is not always the case with human subordinates and their bosses.)

An essential part of your leadership role is to communicate the roles that you intend to play and the role that you expect your follower to play. The role of each participant determines the authorities, responsibilities, and boundaries of the relationship. As experienced human managers understand, anything short of complete understanding or acceptance of each player's role can complicate achieving common goals and often brings individual motivations into question as well. Play your role consistently to keep it strong. Whenever you play multiple roles, for example, both trainer and playmate at different times, you must make it clear which role you are playing in the immediate context that you intend.

Promote effective communication at all times.

In our on-leash walking example, open communications channels included the leash, verbal directions, and visual observation. The leash provided a constant physical channel between trainer and dog as well as a control mechanism. A shared vocabulary of known command cues provided the means to give immediate direction and feedback. Constantly observing the surroundings and upcoming attractions enabled proactive leadership by the walker. Each channel was actively employed throughout the walking conversation.

The best way to promote active communications channels is frequent practice. Engage your follower often in pleasant ways that he enjoys, and whenever he attempts to engage you, always respond in a welcoming way, just as you would a best friend or a favored subordinate in the workplace. Constantly promote his expectation that engaging you properly will always have good consequences.

Cultivating a shared vocabulary requires time and experience interacting with each other. The more expressions, command cues, and context that you share in your daily interactions, the richer the nuance you can convey and, so, the more information you can share through your conversations. Talk to your dog regularly about all kinds of subjects of mutual interest just to keep him engaged. (Actually, almost anything that you talk to your dog about in an engaging manner will interest him if you say it using the right tones.)

Considering the many significant differences between the two species, this prerequisite of sharing a common vocabulary and context presents special challenges to leading a dog at the conversational level. The best solution for this problem is to confine your directing activities as much as possible to those things that you have enough knowledge and vocabulary to direct effectively. As you should know, such responsible deference to the limitations of your knowledge helps when leading human subordinates as well.

With your dog, common things like physical comfort or feelings related to food are examples of where you probably do share sufficient common context to direct him effectively. The more vocabulary you can develop with him through ongoing conversations in these areas, the more easily you can communicate about them.

On the other hand, understanding why your dog might like to sniff other dogs, howl at the moon, or choose to pee in one spot rather than another may require that you obtain additional education about how he thinks in order to direct him intelligently in these matters. The good news is that you may not need to understand so much because, fortunately, you do not need to direct all that many things. In fact, just as in your day job, trying to direct subordinates too much will stifle your ability to lead at any level. You can talk about almost anything but restrict your directing activities only to those areas in which you share sufficient understanding of his motivations and have established a shared vocabulary to lead him effectively in a good way.

Observe and adapt to his behavior.

Once the basics have been properly trained, your main job as a manager is to observe and tune. Conversational leadership requires that you empower your follower to make more of his own decisions and to initiate many if not most of his behaviors without specific direction from you. He must have a significant say in the things that affect him.

In particular, your subordinate must have an acceptable way of politely saying no to you. While refusing a formal command is never an acceptable option for any subordinate, most directives should offer him a way he can suggest that you rethink and possibly withdraw the directive. If you constantly deny the option to suggest alternatives to the unimportant noncommand directions that you give, you risk compromising your ability to engage him in open conversations. Watch for subtle signs that indicate his disagreement with your direction so that you can develop some appropriate signals for him to use as nonconfrontational suggestions for you to reconsider your requests. He will only participate in your conversations if he believes his participation will affect the outcome.

I now offer a personal example of conversing with my dog about his preferences. When I suggest something to my dog that he would prefer not to do, he stretches out his front legs, lowers the front of his body, and looks up at me as his way of saying no. We first learned this protest signal when he used the same body language adamantly to resist my coaxing him to go outside one day when it was raining hard. Because I found it an acceptable signal of refusal under the circumstances, I immediately complied with his request by saying, "Okay," and closing the front door, thereby rescinding my suggestion that he go outside. Through consistent response to this cue when he gives it, we have developed a useful conversational tool. When I accept his protest, I acknowledge so immediately and withdraw my suggestion by saying, "That's okay," or "Never mind." When I do not agree, I strengthen my tone to make clear that I intend a command. Based on his experience, he normally chooses to comply with my formal commands, because he expects that is his best and only choice. However, most situations in which he chooses to protest my noncommand suggestions are just fine with me. My dog makes acceptable decisions a large majority of the time without my need to issue commands, and that keeps him feeling more in control of his life and more at peace with my leadership.

Techniques for Directing at the Conversational Level

At the conversational level, it remains very much the leader's role to direct the activities of his subordinate. That sometimes means providing specific direction in the form of commands. As you grow your leadership skill by intentionally employing conversational techniques, you will want to retain the benefits of commands without the overhead of having to issue them as such. In routine matters, shared expectations, gentle requests, and quiet reminders should usually supplant the need for strict command cues and enforcement. When commands are called for, use these tools in a way that works best at the conversational level; that is, use them in a way that shows respect for your follower and his feelings about what you are commanding him to do.

Maintaining a powerful and effective command repertoire is an essential enabler of the conversational level. In this chapter, we illustrate how to employ good conversational techniques in the same framework that we used to develop our original basic commands.

Look!

Frequent friendly *Look!* requests are powerful enablers of the conversational level. The recommended conversational technique is to practice positive interaction at every opportunity. "Hello!," "Howdy!," "What's up, Bill?," "Hey there, sales star!," and "How is your day going, Mary?" are all easy examples from your work life. Such rapport builders take almost no time, and you can initiate them at will. They focus your subordinate's attention upon you while indicating that an opportunity is available to communicate with you. Putting a cheery tone into your

Look! just makes it even more fun. Say "Hello!" often, and for good effect throw in some other nice sounds that your subordinate will enjoy. A friendly wave or a happy raise of an eyebrow provide convenient visual options for either species. Even if just recognizing the other, frequent acknowledgments build rapport. While it would be inappropriate as an office behavior, I recommend giving your dog a gentle rub behind his ears whenever you walk by just to remind him of your benevolence.

A good measure of your success in building rapport is how often your dependent chooses to give you a *Look!* in hope of getting one back. Leading at the conversational level requires that you accept *Look!* requests from others as easily as you give them. Encourage conversations by initiating friendly exchanges often and by always remaining approachable.

Stop! and *Wait!*

Operating at the conversational level requires your subordinate to embrace your authority and choose to obey even the most annoying of your commands. The restrictive commands of *Stop!* and *Wait!* may be annoying, but they are necessary to establish your ability to control. They must be kept strong and certain because if not, necessary control directives can become opportunities for prolonged conflicts, which will strain your ability to direct conversationally, if at all.

Overusing *Stop!* and *Wait!* commands (other than as quick practice training reinforcement exercises, offering immediate reward opportunities) can put a damper on healthy conversations. However, never fail to give a *Stop!* or *Wait!* when one is appropriate; that would be a mistake. As a competent leader, you must issue and enforce these restrictive directives as commands when needed. Use his name (a priming *Look!* command) and a special tone of voice (firm, not loud) to ensure that he has no doubt that you are indeed giving him a formal command. Always follow up with enforcement, when necessary.

Particularly with these restrictive commands, should you ever recognize that you have issued a command wrongly, always rescind it formally with something like *"Never mind!"* Never let a command that you issue just decay through nonenforcement. If you regularly acknowledge when he is right and take back ill-advised commands when you are wrong, he will communicate with you more readily and obey more compliantly when you need his obedience.

Come! and Withdraw!

The *Come!* invites interaction; the *Withdraw!* discourages it. When using either of these at the conversational level, strive to make your request as gentle and appealing as possible.

When using *Withdraw!* commands to establish boundaries, strive to make the boundary and its impenetrability as clear as possible. Strong boundaries discourage inclinations to cross them and the need for annoying (to both of you) reminders. At the conversational level, when employing a *Withdraw!* command to disengage from your dog, you want it to be heard as welcome permission to go somewhere else or do something else. Offer a quiet "thank you" for compliance and, if you can, offer an indication of when he may re-approach.

At the conversational level, you always want your *Come!* command to be heard as a friendly invitation to join with you. Issue any beck with enthusiasm but softly and respectfully. You may subsequently increase the intensity of your request if gentler requests are ignored and if your motivation warrants, but start as gently as you can. After all, if you are truly leading at the conversational level, your follower should already believe that approaching and submitting to you is something that is good for him, thereby making compliance with your beck something that should not typically require your vehement insistence.

(While it would be an impolite technique with human subordinates, I have a little song I whistle for my dog that I use whenever I wonder where he is or just want him to visit me. I use it only as a suggestion and never as a command. While I have never enforced this cue the way I would a formal *Come!* command, it is usually every bit as effective in getting him to approach. I believe this is because I always reward his response to our special song with a display of unabashed pleasure often brightened by praise and treats, whereas what he thinks I have in mind when I issue the formal *Come!* command may not always seem so appealing to him.

This softer technique also offers an element of absolution, because I do not vary the reward value based on the timeliness of his response to my whistled beck. He knows that while I might admonish him for a late submission to my formal *Come!* command, I always reward his approaching per our special song without further condition or judgment. This little song has also given me a way to ameliorate hard feelings that I may have caused by issuing a command inappropriately, such as perhaps by using an unfriendly tone. I must admit I am still struggling to develop such a gently effective technique that is appropriate for use with humans. I suppose that it may just be a matter of learning to demonstrate patience with humans better.)

As you practice your conversational skills, observe which of your behaviors achieve a compliant approach most frequently and reflect about why each works. Your measure of success in establishing a good relationship is the enthusiasm with which your subordinate approaches in response to your beck.

See! and *Show!*

Because they require so much voluntary cooperation, the *See!* and the *Show!* commands are much more effective at the conversational level. This is why we essentially develop these commands by using techniques for enticing students to choose to comply. By using *See!* and *Show!* frequently in a context that your subordinate finds pleasurable, these become the easiest way to get what you want, usually without needing to give them as formal commands.

(I have many *See!* and *Show!* exchanges that I share with my dog on a regular basis. For example, when I see squirrels in the back yard, I often point them out to my dog, and then we quietly enjoy watching them together. I also encourage my dog to check out new groceries that I bring home as I put them away. We share an understanding that I am letting him examine the groceries up close because he expressed interest but that I am not offering them as food. We understand the routine so well that even fresh meat is not at risk. It is just one more chance to acknowledge and satisfy his curiosity, to encourage him to see things of interest to him, and to let him "show" me that he knows how to behave well in the situation and possibly even get a reward for doing so.)

Learn how to make the things that you want your student to see appear interesting to him. Learn about his natural interests by observing him investigate the things he chooses on his own. Try to incorporate his interests when motivating him to observe your target. An excellent measure of your success with the conversational *See!* is how eagerly your student tries to see the things you encourage him to see.

For leading conversationally, *Show!* is the best command, because when done properly, it offers your student the chance to take the initiative, to participate, and to influence your behavior toward him in a way that he wants. Give him many variations of the *Show!* request frequently and enthusiastically. Make each *Show!* feel like a new opportunity for him to obtain rewards for making the good choice to comply with what he knows you want.

These are two essential best practices to encourage self-sustained conversational "showing":

- Be clear in your mind and in your communications about what you want shown when you make your request. The more lucid and consistent his vision of exactly what your request intends, the more likely you will obtain the behavior you seek.

- Be vigilant about providing the space and freedom that allows him to show you what he is trying to show. Allow your student the autonomy to choose to perform what you ask of him on his own and then give appropriate feedback, especially warranted rewards, when he makes the correct choice.

The ultimate reward at the conversational level is to offer more *Show!* opportunities that allow your follower to show you even more things that he wants to show and that you will reward. Encourage good conversations by rewarding good performance with more opportunities to perform. It is just like rewarding your best salespeople with more hot leads. Any person or dog who is good at doing an activity for which he is rewarded craves more opportunities to perform that activity. A crucial training goal for you is to learn how to let your dog initiate the activities that you want on his own. Once you achieve this, all you have to do is recognize and reward his performance often enough that he feels an incentive to continue trying. At the conversational level, increasing the number of such opportunities to perform is a special reward in its own right.

Nurture Conversational Leadership

Almost everyone seeks low-hassle relationships that provide compatibility, utility, and pleasure. By showing the degree of respect for your follower that is implicit in your use of the conversational approach, you empower your leadership beyond gaining simple obedience. With time and consistency, your student will come to want to do what you want him to do.

It is one thing to develop an environment that enables conversational leadership, but maintaining an ongoing relationship at the conversational level is an ever-evolving challenge that can be quite daunting. The good news is that it is technically simple to do; it only takes focus and discipline. These same attributes of focus and discipline are also, of course, among the most difficult things to maintain throughout your everyday interactions. Nonetheless, you must always be trying.

As the leader, you must nurture your ability to lead at the conversational level by promoting the right activities while avoiding things that can become obstacles to good conversations. Here are the five most important strategic things to do or not to do:

Make Maintaining the Conversational Level Your Top Priority

Always prioritize leading at the conversational level above any other short-term agenda goals. In your professional career, you know better than to let short-term situations cloud the bigger decisions. You avoid career limiting mistakes ("CLM's") even if you don't always sweat the small stuff. You keep your eye on the big prize and do not let the little details blind you.

The quality of the relationship that you have with your dog should always take precedence over any problems you encounter while trying to achieve your immediate objectives with him. So long as you hold the power to direct him conversationally, you will be able, over time, to address any behavioral annoyances readily as well as teach him all kinds of new tricks. To ensure that you maintain this power, always make operating at the conversational level your top priority in every interaction.

Promote Conversational Communications Constantly

Conversational communications are interactive two-way exchanges of useful information. Discussing your subordinate's agenda—his needs and his wants—will encourage his active participation in conversations while also providing you with information that can help you lead him better. Just as with the people you manage, teach your dog to want to tell you things by listening actively and responding appropriately when he does tell you something.

Promote an Active Training Agenda

A good, effective, and intentional training program is one of the most valuable services that any manager can provide for his subordinate or that any owner can do for his dog. Formal training sessions, done properly, are enjoyable exchanges replete with opportunity for rewards that reinforce his happily doing what you want him to do. Training activities offer wonderful opportunities to provide value to your dog through pleasant and useful interaction while it further empowers you to lead him.

In your training sessions, in addition to challenging your student with new concepts, be sure to celebrate material already mastered by frequently drilling and rewarding successful demonstrations of performance. For most intelligent creatures, celebrations of success usually encourage their further pursuit of similar opportunities. These exercises and celebrations take only a few seconds, so do them often.

Deliver on Expectations

Solidly developed expectations are the underpinning of conversational relationships. Specifically, expectations drive the self-selection of "good" behaviors that typifies a well-behaved subordinate. A student's expectations are reinforced or decayed by his actual experience and little else. Consistently reinforce the expectation that if he does what you want him to do, his world will be better. This is the most important expectation that you can nurture. Train this fundamental concept in every interaction. Consistently make it a point to deliver effective consequences that you want to train him to expect: good consequences for good behavior and bad for bad. It is really that simple; just deliver every time what you want him to expect for his actions.

Avoid Obstacles to Good Conversations

As an experienced manager, you know better than to discourage your subordinate's sense of empowerment to pursue his side of the conversation. He must expect that his participation by telling you what he wants is indeed welcomed and expected.

You know to avoid overcontrolling when directing your subordinate's activities, because if you stay too involved and do not let him *show* you his own abilities, you will compromise his internalizing what you are attempting to train. He must take ownership of his behavior.

Wise managers want very self-sufficient subordinates, because it is in a self-directed mode that they can make the greatest contribution with the least effort on the manager's part. Similarly, a wise owner wants his dog to be able to deal with other creatures and situations in an acceptable way without need for his intervention. Any student learns best how to interact properly with others through situations in which he is responsible for his own good behavior, not when he is under external command or control. Teach your dog your rules and then give him the space to show you that he has learned and made your rules his own. Avoid too much meddling, even when he is off target on the nonharmful little things. Give him frequent opportunities to show you things that you request and will reward. On the other hand, when you are not actively leading him with intention, leave him in self-directed mode and avoid excessive intervention in his activities, because that can create unwarranted and unhealthy dependencies.

Be especially careful to avoid soliciting input and then ignoring it. Such behavior is so destructive because it breaks trust that the effort to communicate is useful. Even if you disagree and choose another path, always acknowledge any input you solicit.

Avoid soliciting input that you will confront, unless you have chosen to do so with careful intention. At work, you would never ask a subordinate if he wanted a raise or to take the day off only to refuse his affirmation. However, you probably have seen situations in which a manager has offered a subordinate some responsibility, but when the subordinate accepted the assignment, the manager refused to let that subordinate actually show his ability to perform it. Mixed messages of this kind discourage subordinates from taking ownership of their responsibilities.

This same concept is important with your dog as well. You should never ask your dog if he wants to eat or to go for a walk and then refuse his appropriate enthusiastic response. He won't get the joke. If you ask your dog to show you a behavior and then you fail to give room to perform or if you do not respond to his performance, you tarnish the holy grail of the conversational level, which is his expectation that he can get what he wants by doing what you want him to do. Never do anything to dull that expectation.

Harvest the Benefits

Now that we have completed the training part of this book, and before we move on to our advanced topics, I encourage you to start right now to harvest the benefits of your studies including greater ease of leadership, improved compatibility, and, if you train the necessary skills well, the utility that you want from your student. All of these come from intentional and conscious practice of the techniques that we have just studied. Use them as your normal everyday method of leading your student, and you will strengthen your relationship with every interaction.

Begin, as discussed early in the first section of our book, by reflecting upon and assuming your proper role. As your dog's owner, you are entitled to define the role that you expect of him and to get what you expect, as long as you stay within the boundaries of an appropriately respectful relationship. Your ownership role entitles you to use the tools of rewards and reprimands to mold his behavior. Your ownership role requires you to play the roles of caretaker, manager, and trainer.

Empowerment to perform the roles of manager or trainer must be earned. These roles require the cooperation of your follower, which is motivated by his expectation of consequences. Such expectations can be built only through experience. Start now to build those experiences by consistent application of what you have studied.

If you are getting a new dog, plan well in advance, select him as carefully as you can, prepare his space before you bring him home, and make the impressions on him that you want to make. Do this intentionally from the very beginning.

If you already have a dog, you still can teach him new tricks. While many rules may already be in place through happenstance, you can only get what you want if you pursue training intentionally. We will discuss techniques for changing old rules in the advanced study section, but in the meantime, you should get active and innovative in your conversations with your dog, starting right now. He will respond more quickly than you might imagine. This is easy and even enjoyable to do, once you get used to it. The more you do it, the more benefit you harvest.

Practice observing your dog with the goal of understanding what motivates him. Convince your dog that you are consistently observant and appropriately responsive to his behavior. Give him numerous opportunities to earn what he wants by doing what you want. Through frequent and rewarding exchanges, both parties will learn what is of interest and importance to the other. Each will come to share an understanding of what can and what cannot be done or, perhaps more precisely, what should and what should not be done.

Strive to achieve and sustain the conversational level with your dog through constant focus on reinforcing your relationship. At the conversational level, your dog is more likely to communicate information that can help you to anticipate his needs. Good anticipation minimizes surprises and interruptions. Good anticipation coupled with proactive response keeps small problems small. Urgent interruptions for important things that have gotten out of hand—those most menacing of all managerial crises—occur much less frequently.

Maintain strong mutual expectations to keep your agendas aligned, because, when agendas are on the same path, the amount of energy that a manager must spend on controlling his subordinate is minimized. When the expected outcomes of a potential conflict are already mutually understood, it is not necessary to waste time and emotional energy engaged in that conflict. Teach your student what you want him to learn, and then step back to let him show you what he knows. Directing by choosing from willingly exhibited good behaviors is much less daunting than continually combating bad behaviors.

Perhaps the greatest benefit that one can harvest by leading at the conversational level is simply that it is a lot more fun to interact as collaborators sharing a goal of letting each get what he wants rather than as a boss in a one-sided relationship, pushing buttons to get what only he wants. Your reward will be in the relationship that you create. Go harvest that benefit.

Part Three

RECOMMENDED
ADVANCED STUDY

SELECTED SPECIAL TOPICS

Part Three

SECTION ONE

Adapting for Social Situations

Up to this point, we have been considering simple one-on-one relationships, as in one owner training one dog. As our first advanced topic, we will consider several social situations familiar from our human management lives that we are also likely to encounter as dog owners. These include social environments involving one leader with many dogs, many leaders with one dog, and many leaders with many dogs. Social complexity introduces additional challenges to managing and training that require adaptation by the leaders.

Fortunately, the effective leadership techniques required in socially more complex environments are quite congruent with those for individual relationships. One-on-one relationships are the building blocks of the social fabric, much as individual molecules are the building blocks of substances; they form the chemistry of social interactions. Because of this, we can leverage what we have already learned about leading individual relationships to help us train and manage in socially complex environments.

In order to simplify the presentation of this multifaceted topic, we will confine our application to the relatively simple context of leading canine subordinates and at only one management layer deep. Many of the concepts presented here are, of course, more generally applicable.

Adapting for Multidog Environments

We start our study of socially more complex situations by considering the case of a single owner with more than one dog. Your group may have dogs that are related or that were raised and trained together, or it may contain dogs of many different breeds and upbringings. While your situation with your own set of dogs is unique, all of your dependents share certain common needs and expectations, but each also has unique characteristics requiring your individual attention.

Even among dogs raised together from the same litter, each will have unique personality traits that should be accommodated and enjoyed. Establish a conversational relationship with each individual dog. Feel free to create customized suites of rewards and reprimands tailored to the preferences of each. For the sake of order, however, it is best for all the individuals in the group to share common expectations with respect to important consequences.

The following are essential strategies for leading successfully in multidog environments:

- Satisfy the individual needs of each dog.

- Avoid unnecessary involvement in their peer relationships.

- Channel competitive behaviors to achieve positive results.

- Balance your need for conformity with their desire for individuality.

- Anticipate the training challenges of multidog environments.

- Be aware of pack behavior issues.

We next consider some important details pertinent to each of these strategies:

Satisfy the Individual Needs of Each Dog

Of all the interactions that can arise in multidog social settings, those of a competitive nature have the highest potential for negative impact on you or your pack. Because there is only one of you and many of them, you must apportion your attention throughout the entire group. If you do not give enough attention to any one dog, he must compete harder for it or get what he needs elsewhere. Such competition can induce problematic behavioral dynamics that you very much want to avoid.

An obvious strategy is to reduce the causes for competition by reducing the unsatisfied needs and wants of each dog. In order to do this, you must first know what those are. As part of your training, you need to recognize and then learn to meet each dog's requirements for care and comfort. You must ensure that there are enough of you and the things which you are expected to provide to go around. You may need a process to help you.

As usual, we will jump-start by reflecting on human managerial situations. You probably already use checklists, schedules, and common routines as convenient tools to keep on top of the needs of all of your workplace subordinates. Regular staff meetings, routine status-reporting mechanisms, formal performance tracking procedures, and standardized salary review processes all exemplify how organizations establish routines to help managers take care of employees.

Some similar techniques will work with your dogs, but first, a word of caution. Many organizational processes in the workplace have elaborate lives of their own, often including volumes of procedures for how-to guidance. Unfortunately, much usefulness may be lost because of the amount of process imposed. Avoid going to such extremes with your dogs. To the extent possible, use simple approaches. You will enjoy the process more, will probably do a better job, and can rest assured knowing that your dogs are unlikely to sue you if you make an error in the process.

Create a short written checklist for each dog with his wants, needs, and training goals. Begin by making a list of the issues common to all of them: What do they all want? What do they all need? What behaviors do you want from all of them? What common things do you want all of them to accomplish? What training do you want to give to all of them? Take this list and make a copy for each dog. Then complete each dog's personal list by reflecting on what is unique about that dog's needs. The purpose is to identify the most important agenda topics for ongoing conversations with each dog.

As you create each personalized list, note some things that you might want to bring to his attention through *See!* commands. Be sure to include things that he likes to see to promote keeping that command strong. Note a few things you want him to *Show!* from time to time, behaviors you want to develop in him.

List only a few essential things rather than trying to make your list as encyclopedic as possible. Keep each dog's list to just one page with a few key points. You can always add items as you think of them or delete ones that are no longer useful to you. The exact details that you put on the lists are not so important, as long as you follow a routine for reviewing your lists, thinking about the needs of each dog, and making sure that you address them as you intend. Refer to your lists frequently to keep your intentions and your dog's agenda in the forefront.

Another useful managerial time-lever is to impose schedules of activities on your subordinates. Good things to schedule include those activities you and your group can do best while together. In most organizations, things like group meetings, eating and break times, when to start and end working hours, or when to take vacations are all carefully coordinated to optimize use of time and resources, increase opportunity for desired interaction, and minimize disruptions.

Schedule the most important things but do not bother to schedule unimportant things unless you are concerned that they may be overlooked. (On the other hand, occasionally overlooking unimportant things is not such a terribly bad practice.)

When making a schedule for your dogs, consider which events must be relatively fixed on the schedule, which activities you could slip or eliminate without great problem, which activities your dependents can do at the same time, and which activities must be done separately. Be sure to schedule important occasional activities like visits to the veterinarian and planned times for training.

If you can leverage your time by attending to multiple dogs' needs simultaneously, then by all means, do so. Feeding or walking several dogs together usually works well, but attempting to clean the teeth or trim the nails of several dogs at the same time may not.

Each dog has individual needs that demand separate individual attention, time that cannot be shared. The more demands that you have on your time, the less reliant you must make each dog on receiving individual attention from you. Remember that as a caretaker, you enable and perpetuate dependencies. Accept the dependencies that are inherent with dog ownership, but avoid promoting unnecessary ones.

In your work environment, you ensure additional support mechanisms to provide what your employees need if you cannot personally provide it. In many organizations, you might hire an employee benefits coordinator; with dogs, you may need to hire a dog walker or groomer.

Avoid Unnecessary Involvement in Their Peer Relationships

As an experienced manager, you know that it is a wise practice to identify things with which you will not involve yourself. For example, you know better than to insert yourself needlessly into the peer communications of your subordinates.

Intervention in peer relationships creates dependency, something that is your fault and becomes your ongoing burden. Just as in your work world, intervening in the relationships between your dogs rarely improves anything. Avoid trying to influence peer relationships too much, because in addition to creating unnecessary dependencies, the more you attempt to dictate the social interactions within the group, the more you may obscure learning valuable information while remaining frustrated in your failed attempt to control.

A group of dogs will establish their own arrangement of who sits with whom, where they do so, and who socializes with certain others. Dogs have been making such choices for millennia without owner intervention. Acting as peers, they are quite capable of doing so without you in almost all situations. Manage your individual relationship with each, and let peer social issues be what they will be.

By carefully observing a social setting of several dogs without intervening, you can obtain information about how each dog feels about his social standing. When other dogs are around, each dog may act in ways toward you that he might not act in a one-on-one situation. These behavior shifts will tell you how each dog perceives his relationship with you relative to his perception of the relationships you have with the other dogs. Jealous behaviors indicate insecurities that can precipitate highly inappropriate actions. Be sure to watch for and mitigate the causes for the jealousy. On the other hand, who defers to whom for the honor of sitting next to you reveals their peer dominance rankings within the group, usually without incident or need for any of your involvement.

While you want to avoid needless meddling in peer affairs, it is still crucial that you make it well understood that aggressive behavior toward a peer will cause an immediate unfavorable reaction from you, regardless of the dog or the situation. As their leader, you set the rules of fair competition. You provide value to your group collectively by doing so. You must not tolerate competitive behavior that may be harmful to any member of the group. A strong expectation of a negative reaction from the leader should quash most displays of unhealthy peer competition.

Channel Competitive Behaviors to Achieve Positive Results

Expectation of a strong reaction from the leader can also channel individual competitive urges toward supporting your desired agenda. All intelligent creatures closely observe their peers' interactions with the leader. Whether in pursuit of tangible rewards or for displays of affection, peers in the pack compete to get positive attention from their leader. Employ the technique of public consequences to make the most of your dogs' competitive tendencies and to lead them to supporting your agenda.

Reward good behavior and reprimand undesired behavior publicly. Make it very clear to all observers that good behavior pleases you by your public favorable treatment of performers of good behaviors.

When rewarding publicly, make sure all observers see the reward as something they would want and that, to the best of your ability, they know why you are giving the reward. Be careful that such rewards address a want rather than a need, unless you intend to intensify competitive behavior. A reward to one dog should not be perceived as compromising the basic needs of another, because that could seriously disrupt the social harmony of your pack.

When reprimanding publicly, aim the reprimand unmistakably at the behavior and not at the perpetrator. Never reprimand in a way that might compromise the trust of any observing member of your pack. All pack members will keenly notice a compromise of the trust that they expect of you with any individual member. Your empowerment to lead the pack requires that you maintain their continued trust.

Balance Your Need for Conformity with Their Desire for Individuality

An always important issue that is especially important with multiple dogs is just how much conformity you expect and how much diversity you are willing to tolerate within your pack. Any good manager strives to accept the peculiarities of his subordinates, at least to some degree.

Evaluate the degree of conformity you require for your comfort zone, because if you get outside of that zone, you will find it difficult to lead effectively. Make thoughtful decisions related to your requirements for conformity; you and everyone else in your organization will have to live with those decisions. Keep in mind that diversity tends to take care of itself, whereas demanding conformity requires rules, enforcement, and all the overhead that goes with them. Demands for conformity are like *Come!* commands. Do not use them when you do not need them or when you are not prepared to enforce them relentlessly.

Once you understand your personal needs for conformity, the training needs of your dependents will become more apparent and allow you to choose training approaches that groom individuals who all will fit within your organization the way you want it to be. When you bypass thoughtful evaluation of your needs for conformity, you will let happenstance dictate the level, which can range from stifling uniformity to absolute chaos.

Anticipate the Training Challenges of Multidog Environments

You can simplify the burden of owning more than one dog greatly through common training on subjects such as command cues and expectations of consequence. Imagine if you trained one dog in the group differently by swapping the meaning of the command cues *Come!* and *Wait!* While easy enough to do, it could certainly create some issues of compatibility with the rest of the pack. However, it is easier than may be apparent to elicit quite varied responses from similar stimuli through unintentional training. Such chaos can challenge the peaceful coexistence of human organizations or packs of dogs.

The biggest differences between your human group training experiences and those you will have with dogs are because of differences in intelligence and capacity for self-control. Most dogs, like unsettled youngsters, tend to distract each other and rarely do anything to reinforce the focus of a training opportunity. Because their motivation and attention are more limited, training one by one is usually preferred with dogs, at least when introducing new commands or skills.

Then again, very well managed groups of dogs that are accustomed to performing together can, by group example, reinforce trained behaviors, especially to those dogs lower in the hierarchy. For example, if the dogs are accustomed to sitting quietly and waiting for their food bowls to be filled at eating time, once a new dog is taught this behavior individually, his conforming behavior will be reinforced by the group behavior of the pack. As you have probably observed in your human management experience, peers are extremely good at reinforcing the rules of order that they perceive will benefit them.

Wise managers often employ such peer pressure influences effectively in their organizations. Train each individual and let the pack reinforce en masse the behaviors that you desire through example and peer pressure. The more your dogs expect the consequences that affect them are determined by the pack's overall performance, the more they will encourage the right behaviors in their peers.

Be Aware of Pack Behavior Issues

One special multiple-dog social situation of concern is the potential for pack behavior, especially when the owner or other acknowledged human leader is not present. In most one-on-one cases, a properly domesticated dog will defer to any human as a leader, assuming the human makes a credible attempt at that role. However, when several dogs of a pack are present without an established human leader, they will look to one of their own to be the leader.

Unless your objective is to create some kind of guard dog pack, you should train every one of your dogs to respect human authority, even that of an unfamiliar human. In order to minimize potentially dangerous pack activity, be sure each dog is individually inclined to avoid aggressive behavior. This trait is especially important for dogs that may be exposed to children or similarly defenseless people. You want friendly pack leaders for your group of dogs, just as you want friendly leaders in your workplace who treat your business and your customers well.

Another pack behavior complication occurs when some of the dogs interacting are yours and one or more are not. Like humans, dogs have strong identification with their pack: who is in it as well as who is not. As a wise manager, you would never attempt to direct those outside your line of authority in the same way that you command those in your own group. Doing so has many pitfalls that could erode your image as a leader or confuse the organizational structure, not to mention create peer relationship problems for you with other managers.

In most instances involving multiple packs, you will be the acknowledged leader of your pack, not only by your own dogs, but also by any dogs outside your pack. During inter-pack interactions, the proper role for you to take is as the leader of your own pack. In this way, you are less likely to confuse your dogs by attempting to lead dogs outside their pack—dogs perhaps perceived as members of a competing pack. Avoid confusing the social structure of either pack unless you are acting intentionally to change organizational boundaries.

Adapting for Multileader Environments

Our next social situation is the "many-leaders-to-one-dog" paradigm. A common example occurring in many offices is that of a lone receptionist supporting multiple managers or clients. Another familiar analogy is an only child with two or more parent figures.

An environment with multiple leaders means multiple potential caretakers, managers, and trainers. With more than one potential benefactor, a shared dependent may get some food from one caretaker and other food from another. The same is true for praise, grooming, management, training, or any other item on his agenda. With multiple leaders, the dog has options.

If you have other people living in your home, their mere presence will undoubtedly influence your relationship with your dog. A socially well-adjusted dog should see humans, especially those who are part of his family, as potential managers, trainers, and benefactors. Diminishing your dog's expectation of kind treatment from other humans is a poor alternative, because if you diminish your dog's perception that other humans are good, you will weaken the influence they can have over him, perhaps even to the extent of compromising their safety.

Dogs, as intelligent creatures, will often act autonomously to get what they want. As your dog comes to expect rewards from other humans for doing things that please them, his natural inclination will be to train these additional human caretakers to provide things he wants by trying to please them the way he thinks they want him to please them. A dog's sense of initiative to get whatever he wants from wherever he can is a natural and healthy phenomenon, and often, I think, it is even quite amusing to observe. (Of course, this is not a uniquely canine trait.)

On the other hand, you may not always want so many options available to your dog. Other people in your home may not be conscious of the bad effects of their unintentional training on the behavior of your dog. Most likely, the others in your household have not even read the first part of this book yet!

A multiple-leader environment brings some challenges that demand some special activities by the leadership team. Here are some important ones, with reasons and techniques:

Be Cautious of the Effects of Separating Leadership Roles.

One important activity for the leadership group is to build an awareness of the potential for decoupling the ownership roles of caretaker, manager, and trainer as different people play parts of each role. This decoupling may manifest as a loss of empowerment to perform one role because of not performing another. For example, if one of the other leaders never does the feeding or caregiving activities of a caretaker, he may experience difficulty gaining the empowerment to manage or train. Try to involve each leader in some aspects of each role.

Coordinate the Leadership Group

A coordinated leadership team is essential to remaining in charge of a shared subordinate. The single dog often becomes the boss in a multileader situation by directing other would-be leaders to give him what he wants or needs. Similar to the single subordinate serving many managers in a work situation (like the shared receptionist), the subordinate often comes to define the management pecking order, interface protocols, and priorities of his work activities. After all, when the subordinate is the only one with a complete understanding of his situation, all of his would-be managers are at his mercy.

While much of this "management by subordinates" may seem harmless, it can present a challenge to the authority of managers, individually or as a group. For example, if your family dog is suffering a stomachache from all the treats that he guided another family member to give him, those same treats are not going to serve well as incentives when you conduct your training program.

To stay on top, you have to work with his other leaders. Just as in large human organizations, the leadership team needs to get together from time to time, just to make sure the team is sufficiently consistent with their shared subordinates on the big things.

Appoint a Single "Primary Leader"

In human management situations, experienced leadership teams usually designate a single person to serve as the direct manager of a shared subordinate and to set overall priorities, approve vacations and time off, provide performance reviews, process salary raises, and the like. The choice of this primary leader should be made by the leadership team with intention and not by the happenstance of allowing the subordinate to choose.

The same practice is appropriate for household dogs. Having a primary leader—a designated chief ultimately responsible for the dog— is important for both the household and the dog. Even though many owner and caretaker activities such as feeding, grooming, walking, or training may be shared, the family should confer ultimate control to a specific responsible person.

If the owner or household leadership group fails to designate a primary leader, the dog will make his own choice of caretakers, managers, and trainers. This is not necessarily bad, if you don't mind letting your dog run things. Sometimes, they do just fine! However, if the owners are intent on having management in control to ensure your shared dependent gets everything he needs, then assigning a primary leader is vital.

Promote Consistent Expectations

Another common problem is inconsistency of leadership expectations. Most dogs will tailor their behavior in one-on-one situations to please the particular leader who is present. However, variations in the expected responses from one leader to another can be challenging, if not downright stress inducing, especially when multiple leaders are present and simultaneously promoting different agendas.

Let me share a humorous example from my personal experience. I once trained Lance (our family dog) to sit in a certain corner of our kitchen to wait for his feeding, whereas my son, without my knowledge, trained him to sit by a door several feet from there. At feeding time, if we both were present, Lance would pace nervously back and forth from one spot to another, trying to determine and motivate whoever was going to be feeding him his next meal. When he went to the corner, he would sit and look expectantly at me. If I did not respond, he would go to the spot by the door, sit, and look at my son. He would repeat this nervous pacing from spot to spot in a very apparent angst until he got fed. Fortunately, for all of us, we recognized the situation and learned how to alleviate his anxiety arising from his uncertainty about whom he had to please to get dinner. Now, once we agree, one of us will announce to him as his next feeder so he doesn't have to fret over where to sit to request dinner; he only must accommodate the preference of his designated feeder d' jour.

Every leader character in a dog's life instills certain expectations, often unintentionally. As in the example above, differences may occur from one to another on things the dog considers important, even if the leaders do not. All in the leadership group must consistently train and reinforce common important behaviors to their shared subordinates. While this is important with both species, I think that it may be even more important with dogs, because dogs are usually more dependent.

Promote Consistent Rules and Enforcement

Next to providing for the dog's basic needs, which includes defining his behavioral expectations, the directing manager's greatest responsibility is to train any other possible leaders about what is expected for proper leadership of their shared subordinate.

Those in positions to give rewards and reprimands must share an understanding of what behaviors are desirable and what are not. The dog's expectations for rewards and reprimands from his leaders should be consistent, at least on important behaviors. The more important the rule is, the more important it is that the subordinate's directing manager promotes common enforcement of the rule to all the other leaders.

Adapting for Multidog/ Multileader Environments

Our most complex social situation is that of having multiple dogs and multiple leaders. Having everyone coexist harmoniously in a single organization requires, at a minimum, that the basic needs of each dog be satisfied. The assignment of a primary leader as a resource to each dog in the organization is a key step toward achieving this, because if the primary leader does his job, he will stay on top of what his assigned dependents need and will ensure that he provides for these needs.

In a multidog/multileader environment, much as humans do in a large corporate organization, multiple dogs compete for resources while enjoying a variety of choices about how and from whom they can get what they want. As happens too often in large organizations, the harmony of the management group may be disrupted by competition among the managers for the benefits afforded by having subordinates, or dogs, including the pleasures of controlling them. This element of competition for the attention of shared dogs intensifies the need for cooperation among the potential leaders. The more leaders there are, the more important it is for the leaders to work as a team.

Each leader will likely have his own agenda and preferred interaction style with each dog, at least to some degree. This is natural and good, as long as each leader's agenda is consistent with the owner's overall training plan for the dog.

Effective leadership in this environment requires that each leader show mutual respect for other leaders in his relationships with their shared subordinates. Without such teamwork, the leadership group will compromise its ability to remain in charge. You cannot have one leader sneaking treats under the table to his dog when the team's training plan is to get all the dogs to stop begging for table scraps, just as you cannot have one manager in an office decide to ignore standard company vacation policies as they pertain to his favorite subordinates.

Exceptions to established rules will cause others in the group to interpret such exceptions as opportunities to get what they want, without respect for any other intended order. Such perceived holes in the management fabric are disruptive to the pursuit of common objectives, yet the likelihood of them increases with competition by the managers for the favor of subordinates. If various leaders capriciously apply their own rules, the dogs will pick their leaders according to their perception of who is most likely to give them what they want. This may not serve the intentions of the owners well, and obviously, it does put the dogs in charge.

Dogs are quite capable of differentiating leaders and will exhibit behavior personalized to each one. The natural tendency of a dog to change like a chameleon to please each potential benefactor so he can get what he wants is delightful to most dog-lovers. On the other hand, in many cases, other managers or peers would find such solicitous behavior by a human subordinate to be quite annoying, in spite of it being just as natural. Our expectations of human subordinates should probably be more realistic.

While there may be additional challenges to providing good, effective, and intentional training in a society consisting of many dogs and many leaders, there also are useful formulas for success. Leaders (or potential leaders) who share a common environment should meet regularly to identify the desired behavioral standards, common command cues, and training objectives, and most importantly, to address any unintentional bad training that needs to be avoided or reversed. Developing shared expectations of reward and reprimand is the key to peaceful coexistence, whether one-on-one or many-on-many. Enforcement of a set of common rules by all leaders for all subordinates is the ideal. This achievement becomes possible only when there is common understanding and good teamwork throughout the leadership group.

****

As we close this section dealing with social situations, I reiterate the most important point. As social complexity increases, virtually no special training is required to prepare dogs or other kinds of subordinates. Rather, in each case, such training and adaptation is strictly an issue for those in positions of leadership. In the long run, your dog's actual training and resulting behavior will reflect on the ability of his leadership team to work together.

Part Three

SECTION TWO

Changing the Rules

So far throughout our study, we have enjoyed relatively simple situations of training to instill new rules rather than to change existing ones. As expedient as this idyllic setting has been for exposition, it does not adequately address all of the actual situations in which you train or manage.

Indeed, having the opportunity to select your student or start training from the very beginning is an exceptional luxury that is not available to many managers or dog owners. Moreover, regardless of how you start with your student, someone (maybe even you) almost inevitably provides some unintentional bad training along the way that instills rules of self-guided behavior that need to be changed.

Even if you could train perfectly for a given environment, environments change, often through no fault of the student or the trainer. When the current rules no longer support your agenda, those rules may need to be eliminated or changed.

In this section, we will consider the nature of rules, proper motivations for changing rules, and effective methods for changing them. As in the previous section, we focus primarily on canine applications. I believe that those who have dealt with rule changes in their managerial experience will recognize many of the issues and techniques. Our techniques for changing rules are similar to techniques used in other forms of training, so we can once again leverage what we have already learned.

The Nature of Rules

We open this section with a brief discussion about what rules are and some pertinent aspects of their nature. A rule, as considered here, is simply a conceptual association that is strong enough to influence its beholder's decision-making process. As with any conceptual association, a rule exists uniquely in the mind of its beholder.

Training is a process of instilling the rules by which the student will choose to take a certain self-directed action when faced with a particular situation or stimulus. Good training instills a cohesive set of rules by which the student will choose the desired responses. Good internalized rules like "When I am called, I will approach my caller," or "If I want to be let out, I should tap gently at the door," or "It is never okay to go into Aunt Minnie's bedroom" are built up over time into a fabric that guides virtually every self-directed behavior. Bad rules like "Wait until the parents are gone and then beg the kids for treats," and "I can get scraps off of the table if I move in quickly just after the humans clear the room," and "If I beg and bark loudly enough, I can always get anything I want" also build up over time.

Rules come in many forms and from many sources. While the source creating or trying to create a rule is often external, only those rules that are held internally actually influence the decisions of an intelligent creature.

All intelligent creatures rely upon rules to serve as the framework for processing their decisions. They often even create internal rules for themselves just to simplify their own routine decision-making efforts. Manifestations of self-created rules include things such as repeatedly taking a particular path from one location to another, self-initiated behavioral routines to obtain food or other things, and behaviors exhibited when socializing with other creatures.

The more intelligent or independent your student is, the more likely it is that he will be inclined to make his own rules. This is perfectly natural and fine, provided that the rules he makes are consistent enough with the rules that you would choose for him to make. The fact that his internal rules influence his default behaviors far more than your external rules ever could is exactly why you must constantly align his value system, the source of the rules that he makes for himself, with your agenda throughout all training.

Rules also come from external sources. Among the most powerful rules are the laws of nature, which include things like the immediate effects of gravity or the impenetrability of brick walls. These rules are universally persistent, and attempted violations may be reprimanded vehemently by Mother Nature. Fortunately, these rules of nature are usually intuitive or quickly added to the rule repertoires of most intelligent creatures and need not be taught or changed.

Those who have earned a leadership role provide another important source of external rules. As the leader, you may choose to provide rules within the prerogative of your role. To be an effective leader, you must instill rules promoting your purpose for the relationship. Deciding on a rule you want to make is one thing, instilling it is quite another. Especially with a dog, simply stating a rule is not an effective way to instill it. The rules that your student learns through his observation of consequences will become his real rules, that is, the ones he uses to process his decisions about his behavior. In the parlance of command training, a rule is the same as a standing *Show!* command that your student consistently chooses to obey. A rule is strong when the beholder has a strong internal inclination to obey it.

Proper reasons for imposing your rules include the same as the reasons for doing any training, but most frequently, rules are established to promote compatibility. Strive to maintain a trim inventory of rules that you impose because, like commands, you must persistently enforce every rule that you establish for the sake of all rules. That can be a lot of work. Impose only those rules that you are prepared to enforce fully, and keep in mind that the vast majority of your preferences should not be made into rules that you impose on others, regardless of your ability to do so.

Appropriate rules can be quite valuable, while the wrong rules can detract from pleasure, security, or social order. A primary consideration with every rule you contemplate should be to ensure it is aligned with your intentions, both immediate and long term.

Many rules, especially those made by humans, are highly situational. "Drive on the left side of the road" is an important rule in some countries, yet it would be a terribly dangerous rule to follow in others. Rules of etiquette for greeting a telephone caller may vary depending on whether one is answering his personal phone at home or the business phone at the office. With your dog, while biting a human should always be off limits, licking a human hand could be situational, depending on whose hand and when it is done. Whether your dog must remain submissively on leash or is free to run about depends on where he is and on other issues. The rules that you are most likely to change from time to time are these situation-based rules.

The most effective rules are simple rules. Simpler intellects require simpler rules. Keep the rules that you impose simple by trying to minimize the number of conditions on which your most important rules depend. While simple rules may lack the nuance or refinement of complex rules, they are usually a more effective way of directing the behavior that you want, regardless of the species. The same holds true when changing rules; strive to make rule changes as simple as possible in the eyes of your student.

When to Change the Rules

Strong rules have their effects on behavior, because they are so deeply ingrained. Rule changes, especially ones dealing with important rules, are serious undertakings. They must never be imposed in an immediate reaction to some relatively minor disturbance. The only good reason for you to change any rule that has been established is because the rule no longer promotes behaviors consistent with your agenda.

Good managers change rules with careful intention, because they understand how disconcerting rule changes can be. Good managers never let important rules change without proper planning, if they can possibly avoid it. Rather, good managers follow a steadfast process that begins before they even announce rule changes.

A crucial yet often overlooked preliminary to attempting any rule change is to think through why the old rule is now no longer useful and what the impact of changing it will be. What does not work about the current rule? How did it come into effect in the first place? How important is the rule to your student in his hierarchy of rules? How important is it to change that particular rule? What do you hope to accomplish? What effects, real or perceived, will the rule change have on your subordinate? What are the potential long-term effects of the change on the achievement of your agenda? Are there any potentially undesirable consequences? Changing rules can have serious impacts. Consider the potential effects of the change carefully in advance.

With these cautions in mind, there are indeed situations in which changing the rules is both necessary and good. The most frequent culprits in need of change are rules that have been unintentionally instilled through careless training. Internal rules guide self-selected behaviors. Bad behaviors are manifestations of bad internal rules. Beyond the immediate effects, such bad rules will cause problems for future training efforts if left untreated. You must invalidate and replace bad rules as soon as they manifest in your student's behavior, or else they may impede him in making clear decisions, because lingering bad rules constitute an ongoing influence that conflicts with the good rules.

Another proper reason to change the rules is to adapt to new situations. At work, things like corporate mergers, changes in financial conditions, or changes of organizational focus may require you to establish new rules as a basis for future decision. In times of business change, an ability to change the rules and adapt to suitable new ones often distinguishes the organizational survivors. In your life with your dog, situational changes will also require changing rules through no fault of you or your dog. A new housemate, for example, often calls for changes in territorial rules. Moving or temporarily staying at the home of a friend may also call for some rule changes. Established rules of behavior suitable in open parks or sparsely populated areas may become unacceptable in areas of dense population.

A third and excellent reason to change rules is to eliminate stale, unnecessary rules in order to maintain a trim list of rules. While identifying such useless rules is a healthy ongoing leadership practice, eliminating them can require special care, especially when they have become woven into your student's overall fabric of rules, like a cancer invading otherwise healthy cells.

In the following chapter, we will consider appropriate techniques for both changing old rules to direct different default behaviors and eliminating stale rules.

Techniques for Changing Rules

There are five key steps to making any effective rule change; it is essential that each step be performed and in the proper order:

1. Analyze your intentions for the rule changes vis-à-vis the current situation so that you can tailor your plan to change the rules accordingly. Think through the various implications of the rule change and make sure the new rule is truly aligned with your overall intended agenda.

2. Develop a plan to implement the intended rule changes. Evaluate the effect of the change on your student's expectations and plan to train the rule change accordingly. Only with this insight can you properly apply the fundamental rule of training to help make changing the rule easy and effective.

3. Educate affected parties about your intentions so you can learn from their reactions and tune your plan and intended rule changes as appropriate. Dogs, because of their lower intelligence, have less ability to discern your intentions to change rules through subtle observation. Typically, just telling them that you want to change a rule won't work either. Changing rules for dogs requires being very clear about your intentions.

4. Communicate and implement the new rule clearly and decisively. Provide enthusiastic encouragement of new behaviors contrasted with "different" (nonpositive) consequences to the old behaviors. The difference in the consequences for the old behaviors should depend on how quickly you need to discourage the old rule. When possible, avoid strictly reprimanding old behaviors that were performed with expectations of reward according to the old rule to smooth your student's comfort

with the change. If you rush things too much without allowing adequate time for a proper transition, that could be interpreted as a relationship-compromising affront. Allow for a gradual transition encouraged by emphasis on rewarding the transition.

5. Once a replacement rule has been established, insist on compliance with it from the moment of implementation forward. To internalize and effect the new rule, your student must recognize the change in the consequences that you are providing as intentional and predictable. Use conformance methods to reinforce the change. Watch for your subordinate's compliance, and provide immediate consequences. This is more important when changing rules than it is when introducing new ones, because to replace the old rule, you must make the new rule become stronger than the old one was. As always, tune your reinforcement strategies to obtain the behavior you expect according to your objectives and your student's needs. Be intentionally consistent with consequences you provide in response to observed behaviors as you encourage change.

Whenever replacing an existing rule with a new one, always conscientiously follow the preceding five-step process to promote a smooth transition.

Another excellent reason for changing rules is to eliminate existing unnecessary rules. Unnecessary rules are counterproductive, because they constrain freedom and consume resources to enforce. Routinely hunting down and eliminating useless rules is a highly commendable leadership practice in almost any environment. Observe, however, that changing rules by elimination also requires special care for the sake of the remaining rules.

Consistent failure to enforce a rule will indeed lead to its eventual elimination from your student's portfolio, but such technique creates another problem. Perceived rules that are not enforced can weaken all rules. If you wish to eliminate an obsolete rule, make it clear that while it is no longer a rule, all the other rules are still very much in effect.

Ideally, if the old rule imposes a constraint, you should change it by giving explicit permission to the newly allowed behavior. For example, as an office manager, you should formally announce, "Friday is now casual dress day; business attire is no longer required on Fridays," and not let it just happen through happenstance. Explicitly give the permissions you intend to give. "You are now over 18 years old, and therefore you have my permission to stay out after midnight" does not imply that all rules are being dropped; it simply changes the curfew time rule.

With humans, it is important to communicate the reason you do not enforce what they believe to be a rule. This is because humans are more likely to associate rules and interpret your failure to enforce one as evidence that you may not enforce others. However, with either species, when eliminating a rule, state so and explain why as clearly as possible. Never let a rule simply decay, if you can help it.

Unfortunately with dogs, however, your only viable option for eliminating a rule may be through consistent nonenforcement. When you must eliminate a rule by nonenforcement, try to give specific permission, reward the newly allowed behavior when demonstrated, and enforce all the other ongoing rules vigilantly to minimize any confusion about your intentions.

We will consider some examples of appropriate rule changing situations and techniques as well as an example of this stale rule elimination technique in the next chapter.

Practical Examples

As we conclude this section about changing the rules, I will now offer four examples to illustrate some of the finer points about changing rules effectively:

Example 1: Changing the rules to protect previously unprotected territory.

Example 2: Changing the rules to add a new family member peacefully.

Example 3: Changing bathroom etiquette to encourage a dog accustomed to outdoor access on demand to relieve himself as neatly as possible, inside when appropriate.

Example 4: Eliminating a stale territorial rule.

While the number of possible situations and the rule changes that they indicate is nearly inexhaustible, the approaches illustrated by these four examples should be broadly applicable.

Example 1: Protecting your new carpet

Consider a rule change that you might want to make to protect a lightly colored carpet newly installed in the front hallway of your home. Under previous rules, because you did not care that much about the old flooring, your dog could come in from outside and run right down the hallway whenever you opened the door to let him enter. With the new carpet, you fear he will track dirt and soil it, especially on wet, muddy days. On dry days, however, it may not make much difference to you because his feet do not get dirty or soil your floor. How should you train a change in rules to protect your new rug?

First, you must recognize that the appearance of your new carpet does not have much impact on your dog's decision processes and never will. He may enjoy lying on it because of its soft warmth, or he might even come to learn that all carpeted areas are off-limits if you teach that rule, but the potential for leaving footprint marks will never speak to his sensitivities. The fact that your reaction to his running across your new carpet varies depending on whether or not he is visibly tracking dirt only confuses him, because he is not aware of what is different from one time to the other. If you wish to change the rules, you must create a new rule simple enough for him to understand and strong enough that he is inclined to follow it.

Unlike with animals of greater intelligence (perhaps your children, for instance), you cannot explain to a dog that preserving your carpet is the reason for your new rule. You must base your rule on something that he can recognize. You must teach him a behavior that allows him to recognize a boundary and wait for further clearance to proceed. You can train this easily with basic commands.

Start by defining the threshold of your front door to be an easily recognized boundary. To train your dog to recognize it, point out the doorway threshold repeatedly and never let him enter without your specific permission. Every time he approaches it, have him stop, sit, and wait for your permission to advance. Scold him gently if he ignores the new rule, and make him go back out and wait for your permission outside the door for an amount of time that he finds annoying. When he does enter after securing your permission, praise him.

With very consistent reminding and copious positive reinforcement when he complies with the new rule, you train him to pause at the door as a standard default behavior. This will give you an opportunity to inspect and clean his feet before he enters and thereby get what you want from the rule: a cleaner carpet. While you might wish him to recognize when his feet are dirty, this is not a realistic option, so you just have to adjust to his limitations and train him to defer to you to decide when he may enter.

Example 2: Bringing a new dog into the family

We next look at an example of changing the rules for the first dog such as required when introducing a second dog into your home. A new dog requires rule changes for the first dog related to territorial things, including sharing toys and interaction with the owners. It may also require learning new rules of interaction with a peer.

A familiar analogous situation in your work environment would be when adding a second receptionist to your organization. The first receptionist will likely perceive both benefits and concerns. Perceived benefits may include having a friendly work associate and having additional help in doing the required tasks around the office. Probable concerns center around sharing a territorial workspace, such as the reception desk, perhaps even some annoying things like contamination by another's germs on his phone's mouthpiece, and certainly some big things like competition for the favor of the boss or fear of falling down in the office pecking order. Depending on the reasons that the first receptionist perceives that you are bringing in the new one, he may also feel some concerns about job security with the visible addition of his potential replacement.

As the manager in this situation, the rules you will need to change may involve work hours, seating assignments, and work task responsibilities. You will also need to add some new rules to clarify the relationship you expect between the two of them.

As a thoughtful manager and assuming that you intend to continue a good relationship with the first receptionist, you would have discussed your intentions to get a second receptionist well before doing so. You would do so with clarity of purpose and a vision of your intention for their eventual working relationship. As you address these issues with your first receptionist, you would clarify and strengthen your mutual understanding of what you each consider important. You would try to sell the advantages and mitigate the potential concerns, much as you would train any new behavior. You would want to develop the new rules with your original receptionist in the relatively safe harbor of your one-on-one relationship in order to instill a sense of comfort and, ideally, ownership of the new rules when the new person comes on board.

Similar techniques work very well when changing the rules as you introduce a second dog into your home. Your initial focus should be on strengthening your relationship with your existing dog. By reinforcing what things are his and his territorial rights, and addressing his natural concerns about having to compete for what he needs from you, you prepare him for the change. Naturally, with his lower intelligence, you will not be able to communicate with him what the change is going to be as you might with your receptionist. Nonetheless, in either case, the first step is to clarify and strengthen those rules that you already have in effect and that will continue after the change.

The second step is to introduce and begin training the new rules before they become necessary. With your receptionist, you discuss and build agreement and acceptance of the changing situation and expectations. Ideally, you would gain your receptionist's buy-in through involvement in the decisions about the new rules such as rules about seating location, work hours, or other things of importance to him. You want the new rules understood in advance of introducing a new peer. The fewer rules you need to change at one time, the easier it will be.

In your dog's case, this second step is not as easy to do directly. The most you can do in advance is to reinforce his comfort that you will meet his needs and give him the attention that he wants. He needs to have some things of his own that he knows are his. Make sure he feels comfortably in control of the things about which he will become territorial. Make sure he has a food bowl of his own as well as a blanket or sleeping place he knows is his.

While you will want to provide a similar set of things to your new dog when you get him, do not bring them in too soon, or your first dog may add them to what he considers his own prized possessions. You will not want to take anything away from your old dog when you introduce the new one, so do not give him any new things that will not remain his.

The third step in changing these rules is to introduce the new situation while firmly reinforcing both new and continuing rules. With your first receptionist, this means continuing to involve him in decisions that affect him after the new receptionist arrives. With your dog, it means confirming what is his and that you are still giving him everything he expects from you. It also requires being clear about the territorial rights of the new dog. His bowl is his bowl, his blanket is his blanket, and so forth. Establish from the very beginning the boundaries and your expectations for friendly, compatible behavior.

The more your old dog is comfortable with what is his, the more likely he will respect the new dog and not compete for his possessions. The less comfortable he is about what is his, the more likely the ugly side of competitive behavior will appear. (Based on my experience, if one is not careful about ensuring territorial satisfaction, introducing a second dog may be more similar to introducing another commissioned salesperson into the same territory than it is of introducing a second receptionist into an office.)

One last comment relative to this new dog example is in order. Once the dogs are properly introduced and comfortable with the definition of their respective territorial rights, be sure to avoid trying to control their peer relationship. This is something best left to them, at least so long as it stays within your rules for fair competition or, at the very minimum, nonviolent coexistence. Do not make or try to enforce rules of peer interaction that are not necessary or warranted. That is something best left to your dogs.

Example 3: Changing Bathroom Privileges

Sometimes, simple changes in his owner's routine can require difficult changes to the rules for a dog. Consider a change of situation in which you must start being away from home for prolonged periods, which causes you to need to restrict your dog to staying indoors while you are gone. While capacities may vary, he probably will need a permissible area inside where he can relieve himself. Before the change in situation, when you were not gone for prolonged periods, you could let him out in the yard on his demand frequently enough for his needs. He knew to tell you of his need and expected a strong reprimand should he not go outside before starting to do his business. In the new situation, you would like to train a new rule about where in the house he has permission to go without sanctioning that he may go anywhere or any time that he is inside the house.

To effect the change, you must identify and communicate new information about where he may go in a series of carefully planned steps. First, put newspapers or another discernable target down in the place you want him to go. Next, get him to use the papers by not letting him out when he signals to you that he needs to go out and redirect him to the new target area. Restrict him to the area so he has no choice other than to use the papers, and then praise him lavishly for doing what previously was a forbidden act. This will be very confusing and uncomfortable to him at first, but with consistent reinforcement, he will eventually learn to perform.

You can only effect such a complex change in the rules through a careful change in the consequences that you provide to your dog's behavior. With a lot of practice, you will change his bathroom rules to say, "Go outside whenever you can find someone to let you out, but if you see the papers are down and no one is letting you out, use the papers, and you will be rewarded." After a while, by putting down papers only when you will be gone for a long time, you will get the behavior change you are really seeking as he learns to understand your new rules as you intend them to be.

Example 4: Changing an "Off-Limits" Room back to "On-Limits"

Suppose your aunt who is afraid of dogs no longer lives in your home, and you now want it to be okay for your dog to play in the previously off-limits living room. This situation requires that you employ the "stale rule elimination technique" to make the change.

Begin by going into the living room yourself, explicitly inviting him to come to you, and then praising him for being there with you. Depending on how well the off-limits rule was instilled, he may be respond with hesitation to your beck. If he resists, be sure to allow time for the adjustment. In particular, this is one situation when you should not reprimand him for not coming per your beck, even if you made the mistake of issuing your initial invitation into the previously forbidden space as a formal *Come!* command.

Hesitation on an established command normally indicates that your dog may be going through stress-inducing inner conflict caused by two opposing rules that you have taught him and that he has adopted. You need to make one rule win and the other lose. As with humans, temptation can be a very useful tool in accomplishing this. Just have visible treats available in your hand when you invite him and ensure that your beck is as gentle, friendly, and encouraging as possible. Then, once he crosses the forbidden threshold, treat him and praise him and encourage him to stay with you for a while. After a few minutes, encourage him to stay while you leave the room. If he stays, you are well on your way to having established the rule change. If he runs out with you, repeat the routine often over several days. Soon, your living room may become a regular stop on his tour of your home as the old rule fades and he loses his sense of discomfort.

At the same time that you are eliminating that living room restriction, be extra vigilant about enforcing any remaining territorial restrictions you intend to keep. This will minimize any corruption of the rules that you want to keep while you eliminate the intended rule.

Part Three

SECTION THREE

Dealing with Personalities

Many years ago, while employed as a senior vice president of a large corporation, I sought the counsel of my boss about how to deal with a disruptive personality conflict between two of my departmental directors. As I began to explain the situation, he closed his eyes for a moment, let out a long frustrated sigh, and then leaned forward to coach me in a slow, tired, deliberate voice: "As a manager, the last thing in the world you ever want to deal with is personalities. I would think you should know that by now. What else would you like to talk about?"

Perhaps that admonishment has led me to place this material about dealing with personalities so late in the book. Over the years, I have often pondered whether the counsel of this seasoned executive emanated from the wisdom of his experience or the tired cynicism often accrued from too many years of corporate life. While I understand that a manager certainly does not want to become involved in personality conflicts if he can avoid it, I have found that effective leaders do deal with personalities and associated issues when they must. (When speaking of issues with personalities, we typically mean problems with personalities, because without perceived problems, most personalities are pleasantly translucent and warrant little training or adjustment.)

An additional reason for my heretofore reticence to address topics related to personality is that there are many books and articles written about the theory of personalities. Many thoughtful authors have written about issues with personalities, as well as techniques for dealing with them. Through popular seminars and books, many seasoned managers are already well-acquainted with elaborate systems for analyzing personalities.

Most of these systems offer suggested techniques using named personality styles, numeric grids, or color charts based on various attributes such as assertiveness, responsiveness, inclination to trust others, goal-pursuit orientation, and so on. If you have never looked into such systems, I suggest you do so. Dogs, like people, vary widely in these same personality traits, and many of the techniques prescribed by these systems are quite applicable to dogs.

Abstracting from the myriad systems for dealing with personalities that I have studied, I find two key observations that are promoted by virtually all of them:

- We observe the personality traits of others in the context of our own personality and social expectations.

- Effectively dealing with personalities requires substantial observation, introspection, and self-control to manage one's own behavior responsively to the personalities of others.

Some may perceive one person as too aggressive, while others may find the same person too reticent. What seems rude in one society may be perfectly acceptable in another. One not expecting a friendly overture may take it as an unwelcome intrusion. For example, my son is far more welcoming of our dog jumping up and licking his face than is my wife. (Our dog understands this and conducts his shows of affection discriminately. I think such discretion is a mark of a well-socialized personality.)

While many issues of personality transcend the species, happily for our purpose of dog training, a dog's personality is much simpler than that of a human. Dogs hold fewer rules and process them even less. Moreover, one can and may usually do far more to train the personality of one's dog than one ever should attempt when dealing with the personalities of one's workplace associates. Therefore, we will confine our focus to personality issues with dogs that may be reminiscent of issues observed in your managerial experience. Of course, much of what we will study about dealing with the personalities of dogs is more broadly applicable.

A Brief Model of Personality

We start by considering a model of personalities as they are driven, manifested, and observed. Three distinct facets (the *inner personality*, the *manifest personality*, and the *perceived personality*) together make up what we call the personality of an observed intelligent creature.

The Inner Personality

The *inner personality* is the internal control program of a creature's mind. The inner personality interprets information and drives basic behavior; it evaluates opportunities and selects the actions that it expects will provide benefit. Analysis of whether the inner personality is neurologically hard-wired or just deeply embedded through early and persistent learning is far beyond our scope here. For our purposes, we may assume that, once developed, this core is virtually immutable.

The purpose of the inner personality is to promote survival by directing actions that satisfy needs, especially those believed necessary for survival. Different inner personalities are simply different control programs running with different sets of expectations (decision processing rules, if you will) and on "hardware" unique to the creature that possesses it. What could there possibly be not to like about an inner personality, unless another's program for survival threatens your own?

The Manifest Personality

The second facet of personality, the *manifest personality*, is "showing" behavior motivated by the natural inclinations of one's inner personality to get what one wants from social interactions with others. Manifest

226

personality is observable through styles of interaction and regimens like manners.

Although heavily influenced by the inner personality, the manifest personality is in large part learned behavior. Whether through happenstance or intentional training, intelligent creatures learn to conduct their interactions with others in a way that they believe supports their own agenda. Like all learned behaviors, the manifest personality comes from conceptual associations instilled by observation. The manifest personality is based upon rules, although upon which rules is not always apparent.

Most intelligent creatures vary their manifest personality traits according to whom they are interacting with, because they have learned the benefits of doing so. For example, one may manifest aggressive tendencies with those perceived to be competitors, whereas the same creature may manifest much more gentle behavior with those considered family. Through the first manifestation, territory can be protected, and through the second, nurturing can be given.

The more intelligent and discerning that a creature is of others, the more likely it is that he will intentionally try to adapt his manifest personality. That is why humans are usually more aware of their manifest personalities than are canines, although well-socialized canines can certainly be highly discerning in their manifest personalities.

Because of their presumably higher intelligence or level of education, we should expect trainers and managers to be more capable of adjusting their own manifest personalities than their students, subordinates, or dogs. This ability to stay in control of what behaviors one manifests is of primary importance when dealing with personalities.

The Perceived Personality

The third facet, the *perceived personality*, is the personality as observed by another, which is a composite of manifest personality traits as seen through and interpreted by the observer's inner personality. Each of us perceives personality traits that are manifested by others relative to our own inner personalities.

While you can do little directly about the personality that you perceive in others, other than to engage it, strive to remain keenly aware of how your own inner personality can filter and even distort your observations of another creature's manifest personality. When seeking to understand another's perceived personality, reflect on your own personality's characteristics as well as your subject's motivations to manifest the traits that you perceive.

****

One final item in this brief primer is a reminder that your manifest personality is perceived through the filters of the creature observing it. When those you are presuming to lead do not react as you expect, you must adapt your manifest personality to stay in charge. After all, your manifest personality is really the only aspect of the personality perceived by others that you can control. Happily, your higher intelligence and self-control should give you a readily sustainable advantage in creating the perceptions that you want your dog to have of you.

Training Personality

Before considering an attempt to train another's personality, contemplate the proper responsibilities of your role as well as the proper limits on your authority to do so. As a manager, you know better than to attempt to train the inner personality of a workplace subordinate. It is simply not your place to do so, even if you could. On the other hand, as a caretaker for those in your organization, you have responsibility to maintain social order, which means you may impose behavioral boundaries on the *manifest* personalities of your workplace subordinates.

As the owner of your dog, you have the responsibility and the prerogative to train any parts of his personality that he needs to live harmoniously in the society to which you introduce him. You owe such care to your dog and everyone with whom he comes into contact simply because you are his owner. Shaping the personality of your dog may well be one of the most challenging yet important requirements of you as an owner. It requires training at its best, which is achieved in four parts:

1. Be clear about your purpose.
    (Know what personality traits you are seeking and why.)

2. Recognize his basic motivations and needs.
    (These drive the inner aspects of his personality.)

3. Consistently deliver effective consequences to observed manifestations of personality.
    (The fundamental tool.)

4. Continually tune your approach as his personality develops.
    (The Fundamental Rule.)

As you train personality traits, you will be most effective if you consider and strive to accommodate the inner personality needs of your student at all times. This, more than anything else, is what drives him to manifest what he does.

Unless you are a dog breeder, it is unlikely that you will own your dog at the earliest developmental stages of his inner personality. If you have a choice, get your dog from a place that has afforded him the kind of humane and gentle treatment that you want him to manifest; such traits are deeply rooted. Any further personality training you do will rest on this base. It is much like selecting employees who already have the right basic values and social skills. Some things you can improve through training, but other things are too close to the core to do much about. (I recognize expert trainers can and have done much to rehabilitate dogs that have been treated inhumanely. However, doing so can be quite challenging for those without such special expertise.)

The best personality training you can do for your dog is to train him to manifest personality traits toward others that will make it easier for him to coexist harmoniously. Many of these positive manifestations are what we call good manners.

Avoid inclinations to shape your student's personality into a mirror of your own personality. Enough of this will happen naturally. Recognize that the personality of your student is his personal control program, one that drives his reactions to his environment as he sees it. Recognize that part of his personality came hard-wired and that you have to work around that core. If you are able and willing to accommodate the shortcomings of his personality, you will provide great value to him in your relationship. Said another way, if you adapt effectively to your dog's personality, it will be easier for you to lead him.

Some Common Personality Issues

Issues observed in a manifest personality may simply be a problem with the way you perceive your dog's personality, or they may indeed be the result of problems that he actually has.

The path to a proper resolution of an actual problem starts by determining the source of the issue. Usually, personality problems come from bad rules, that is, internal rules that arise from erroneous expectations that promote flawed behavior. Once these erroneous rules have been identified, they can be changed appropriately.

In the case of any perceived personality problem, consider first that the problem may stem from an expectation that you hold that may be unreasonable. If this is so, the solution is for you to reassess your expectations and to identify reasonable accommodations that you can make.

Otherwise, the problem that you perceive comes from an expectation held by your dog that some needs of his might go unsatisfied if he does not display the aberrant behavior that manifests his personality issue. To address this kind of problem, you must first identify the issue motivating his behavior and acknowledge that his need is indeed real to your dependent. Then you can find a way to change his internal rules by teaching him new, stronger rules by which he can achieve satisfaction of his need. Whether it is safety or food or some other need, you must teach him there are acceptable behaviors through which he can get what he is seeking without misbehaving, and at the same time, you must teach him that he will never get what he is seeking through his continued aberrant behavior.

We next demonstrate how to apply simple rule-changing techniques in the context of specific personality issues through the examples that follow.

Aggressive Behavior

Before seeking to address aggressive personality traits, take care to distinguish aggressive behavior from merely assertive behavior, which, in contrast, can be very desirable. It is perfectly natural that intelligent creatures will seek to attain the things they want. The difference is that aggressive behavior is an attempt to control without respecting established rules for interaction, whereas assertive behavior intends to attain what one wants within a socially acceptable framework.

As always, the best way to discourage the development of aggressive behavior is by addressing your dependent's desires proactively before an issue develops. Always treat your dog with respect for his security. Protect him from the overly aggressive behaviors of others. Strive to be aware of what frightens him and minimize its effect on him. Observe for cues that set off his aggressive behavior. Sometimes they are obvious, but they may be as subtle as a person wearing a piece of clothing that your dog associates with a bad experience. In serious cases, you should consult a professional dog behaviorist.

Maintain and enforce clear boundaries between acceptably assertive and unacceptably aggressive behavior, first in your own mind and then instill them in your student. Differentiate the rewards and reprimands that you provide sharply at those boundaries. Acknowledge polite overtures instantly, and strive to satisfy his wants as soon as practical after he manifests that acceptable requesting behavior. Conversely, always firmly reprimand inappropriately aggressive behavior immediately. Set the line, and keep it clear.

The tendency to aggressive behavior usually indicates a predisposition to expect threats to one's well-being. Displays of aggressive behavior are often pre-emptive strikes motivated by an expectation of denial of some basic need such as food or safety.

Regardless of the reason, it is an essential responsibility of anyone leading a dog to confront displays of aggressive behavior immediately and forcefully. By forcefully, I mean to act in a calm yet highly assertive manner while imposing your control. Avoid confronting him with aggressive behavior of your own. While your reactive show of aggression may instill fear and get instant results, they encourage your dog's use of aggression as a default behavior when he needs to assert himself. The smarter your dog is, the more he will mirror your methods.

In order to discourage aggression, never allow your dog's aggressive behavior to achieve what he wants, particularly desires related to basic drives such as safety or food. If aggressive confrontations do occur, minimize their duration through immediate forceful intervention. Never let sustained aggression achieve the reward of a win, as this will only teach that aggression is a viable tactic.

For example, should your dog fight aggressively for a bone or a toy of some kind and he gets it, never let him keep it. Command a *Drop!* and then put his winnings away for a long time.

While a *Stop!* is an obvious command choice to employ when countermanding aggressive behavior, remember that the better technique is to suggest acceptable alternative behaviors through which your subordinate may achieve what he is seeking or, at a minimum, distract him from the target of his aggression by rewarding and praising him for staying inside the lines.

Build social compatibility by constantly reinforcing your student's internal rule that appropriate, gentle, assertive attempts and gentle play with others is the best route to getting whatever he wants by rewarding them quickly. Provide many opportunities through which nonaggressive, friendly, and polite interaction will easily allow him to achieve the rewards he seeks, and he will adopt nonaggression as a good behavior in his value system.

Needy, Clinging, and Begging Behavior

Needy, clinging, and begging behaviors are attempts by the perpetrator to get what he wants without fair regard for you or the prerogatives of others. The only way to change such personality flaws is to combat them, much like you should deal with openly aggressive behavior.

While not as dangerous as openly aggressive behaviors, excessive demands for attention can be quite annoying, if not disruptive. Such behaviors can compromise the harmony within organizations, especially when competition for resources such as managerial attention is intense. Needy, clinging, and begging behavior is a form of aggression channeled into manifestations that may appear to be more palatable than wantonly aggressive behavior. Although they should, managers or peers often do not confront such manifestations of neediness the way they would unbridled aggression.

To address such behavior, first determine what is driving the individual to exhibit the needy behavior. What does he really want? Is he seeking attention or recognition from you or someone else? Is he seeking protection from someone or something? Is he pursing a desired reward through bad behavior because he learned that persistent pursuit of such bad behavior sometimes works?

Next, determine whether you should satisfy his desire. Is it something to which he is entitled? While it is not your place as a manager to determine the legitimacy of certain pursuits of your human subordinates, as an owner, you certainly have the prerogative to decide what is appropriate for your dog to pursue.

If you determine you wish to provide the satisfaction he is seeking, do so only when he is not begging. Try to anticipate the need that is motivating the begging and satiate it. You may use his begging as an opportunity to learn what he wants, but never accept it as a cue to satisfy his request. Make it a point to provide what he wants only when he is not begging, and you will remove any reason for him ever to beg to get what he wants. This is exactly as it is with humans, whether they are seeking more money, acknowledgment, recognition, or a chance to show you something. You need to remain in control of your decision to provide what your student wants and to give in only when his request is appropriately made.

For example, if your dog rudely interrupts you, begging for attention and petting, rebuff him with a *Stop!* or *Withdraw!* Later, sometime after he has disengaged fully from begging, call him to approach you and pet him lavishly until he tires of it. Similarly, feed him on a regular schedule and according to his needs. Do not make him beg for food; make his feeding a reliable routine. If he begs for food because it is almost feeding time, suggest a *Wait!* or *Soon!* and then, after a brief period of disengagement, reward him for his sustained compliant waiting; do not reward his begging. Even when he is begging to be let out for relief, train him to ask you in polite ways.

Teach your student the difference between properly asking and improperly begging by watching for what you consider proper requests and quickly satisfying them. If you reward any aggressive begging, you will teach that aggressive begging works and that it is only a matter of how much aggression is required to get what is wanted.

With respect to treats, which are a frequent target of begging behavior, make it a point to create situations where your dog can earn treats by showing certain behaviors that you request him to show. Learning how he can get treats by doing things you ask of him alleviates his need to beg for treats. Teach him to initiate getting treats by doing so in a way you will enjoy. (I like my dog to use gentle *See!* requests of me through which he tries to lead me to where his treats are stored. When my dog persists in politely seeking what I consider an excessive amount of treats, I usually offer him a training session as an alternative and then give him treats when he has demonstrated the tricks that I request of him. This also helps me feel like I am staying in charge.)

Excessive Barking

Most people, especially experienced managers, are familiar with the disruptive effects of people with personalities who seem to do a lot of growling and barking, often with little apparent reason. Although most people do it occasionally, constantly creating excessive amounts of noise is a personality problem that can be quite disruptive.

While it varies among canines, often by breed, a certain amount of barking is part of every dog's nature. Whether in the role of an owner or a manager, you are the one who must decide what is too much barking and what is not, taking all the causes and effects of the barking into consideration.

As in addressing other personality issues, the first thing to do before seeking to change barking behavior is to reflect on what makes you think the situation even needs to be addressed. It may be that you are too intolerant of the natural behaviors of others. If so, you must attempt to correct this problem, because such excessive intolerance can be a debilitating personality issue. To fix it, first recognize that like all personality issues that you manifest, the problem likely stems from some unmet need of yours.

However, if after due reflection you still determine that the personality issue is with him and that you must do something to address his excessive barking, then the next step is to determine why he is barking. What motivates him to do it?

Typically, a dog barks to satisfy a need to communicate something. Your dog may be trying to draw attention to him or something he wants others (often you) to observe. Respond to this assertive *Look!* or *See!* request in a way that encourages him to show you what he wants you to see in a way that you find more acceptable. Encourage him to be quiet in a soothing way, and then reward his continued silence by quietly encouraging him to show you what he wants you to see.

Teach him appropriate ways to get your attention by using cues to which you will readily respond without becoming upset. If you respond to a single bark or to his showing excitement in an even quieter way, he will have nothing further to gain by continued barking, as he will likely risk a reprimand for his loud noises. If he ever does get what he wants from incessant barking, this will bolster his irritating tendency to bark until he gets what he wants. Again, nothing encourages a behavior, good or bad, like the success of getting what is sought.

A common reason for a dog barking aggressively is that he feels a need to protect himself or his pack. While this form of aggressive behavior may seem justified sometimes, you should discourage it as you would any aggressive behavior. If you find that his concern for his safety is warranted, then look for ways to address his concerns other than responding to his aggressive barking. Distract him with some requests to show you calm behaviors that he knows, like sitting or lying down. Protect him proactively if necessary by removing him from the situation or removing the source of his concern as is appropriate to your caretaker role.

Regardless of what motivates excessive barking, the good news is that dogs almost always stop barking when they get what they want. (One can only wish that people were the same way.)

Overly Timid Behavior

Sometimes called "scaredy-cat" behavior, I have found that humans and dogs are more likely to manifest such seemingly irrational fearful behavior than felines are. Scaredy-cat behavior is not a dangerous problem like aggressive behavior, nor is it as annoying as begging or barking too much, although sometimes it does lead to these behaviors. However, such a scaredy-cat personality trait can keep a person or a dog from being all he can be.

With overly timid behavior, the first and most important thing to reflect upon is whether your dependent is truly manifesting the trait to an abnormal degree. What you may perceive as being overly timid may just be your student staying true to his inner personality and trying to remain in what he believes to be a sensible comfort zone.

The worst thing you can do when dealing with what you take for overly timid behavior is to treat your dependent's fears as unfounded. Fear is a core driver of the inner personality; it is not simply a manifest personality trait. While you may not share his fears, he learned them somehow, and they are very real to him. Otherwise, he would not be manifesting the overly timid behavior. To address the issue, you must find the cause for the fear and deal with that.

An irrational fear is an incorrect conceptual association that implies an uncomfortable consequence from a stimulus that does not actually cause such a consequence. It is an erroneous rule. The way to address an erroneous rule is to replace it with a rule that associates the stimulus of the fear with a consequence that is good (or, at worst, neutral). You can do this as described in the chapter on changing the rules, but do so with great care because rules that drive fear, whether rational or irrational, are usually woven deep in the fabric of one's personality.

Above all, before you endeavor to instill such a rule change, be cognizant of which rules are within your prerogative to change and which are not. Some fears are appropriate for your student's well-being, even if you do not share them. A good trainer always places a higher value on his student's well-being than he does on less important training goals.

Conclusions about Dealing with Personalities

Any personality issue can become self-reinforcing and increasingly pronounced if the aberrant behavior manifested achieves rewards. Rewards can include things like treats as well as expected (but undelivered) reprimands. Aggressive behavior that wins a reward teaches that aggressive behavior can be an effective tactic. Begging behavior rewarded with treats does likewise. When incessant barking achieves the results that less intrusive calls for attention do not achieve, incessant barking becomes learned as an effective technique. Nothing reinforces any behavior like success.

To address a personality issue with an intelligent creature of any species, you must change the rules that your student is using to drive his personality. Like any bad rules, you should fix them whenever it is within your role and your ability to do so. The trick is to satisfy your dependent's needs through proactive routines and never because of demonstrations of his personality issues."

Above all, remember that when dealing with personalities, expending an effort to adjust your own manifest personality is much more likely to produce the results you want than will any attempt to change another's personality directly. When dealing with personality issues that are crucial, use what you have learned to cause the needed change, but when dealing with matters that are not so important, choose the easier route of accommodating your student's personality in your one-on-one interactions. This will let you provide value and thereby keep your dog happy that you are in charge. The best leaders get their greatest power to lead because their followers want to follow them. When your dog's personality manifests that he wants to follow your lead, you have indeed trained him well.

A FEW CLOSING COMMENTS

IN CONTEMPLATION OF DOG OWNERSHIP

A DIFFERENT PERSPECTIVE
ON OWNERSHIP

SIMILARITIES AND DIFFERENCES

Congratulations! You have now completed the entire training program offered by this book. Whether you were just looking for some ideas about training your dog or were reading to pick up some new insights for managing other intelligent creatures, I hope that you have enjoyed your reading, and in particular, I hope that you will find useful applications for what you have learned through your efforts.

In this section, I address some motivations for getting a dog of your own as well as your dog's likely perspective on what he wants in his owner, and finally, I close with a review many similarities followed by several important distinctions that differentiate appropriate leadership of humans from that of canines.

In Contemplation of Dog Ownership

This chapter is especially for you good managers who may be contemplating taking on ownership of a dog. If you are comfortable with the leadership philosophies espoused in this book and meet a few other qualifications, then I would encourage you to get a dog of your own.

Recognize that dog ownership will require you to assume responsibility for a totally dependent new friend. You will owe him caring application of your best management skills to ensure that his needs are always satisfied. You must commit to this as you would any serious leadership undertaking.

Visualize your role in your dog's life and his role in your life. Plan the boundaries you will place on him. Visualize how you will schedule his feeding regimen, his exercise routines, and his training activities. Address management matters with any others who will share his home. Good dog owners, like good managers, set objectives for care, management, and training and then, guided by those objectives, implement an effective plan to accomplish those objectives.

If you have made the commitment to be a good owner and have a developed a well-considered plan, owning a dog will offer you many splendid opportunities for pleasure and satisfaction. Furthermore, your dog just may help you become better at your day job. Here are a few examples of how:

A dog will demand some healthy routine in your life away from work.

Many managers apply their planning and scheduling skills almost exclusively to their career organization, while neglecting such activities in their personal lives. Owning a dog can encourage a better balance and more enjoyable use of your discretionary time away from work.

A dog has simpler needs than most people.

Good managers strive to help those for whom they are responsible get what they seek. Your dog will provide you with many easy opportunities to satisfy him while offering delightful respite from the complexities of satisfying all the people in your professional life. Learning to recognize and satisfy simple needs will make you a better manager and a happier one, as well.

A dog offers healthy opportunities to "overmanage."

While most managers need involvement and control, many tend to overmanage, to delve into too much detail, or to attempt to exert too much control. This misplaced activity stems from a natural drive for the satisfaction of gaining immediate responses to attempts to direct the actions of others. While getting immediate responses to one's detailed directions is rewarding, seeking too much of this can weaken a manager's effectiveness with human subordinates. However, a dog of your own can offer many good outlets for dissipating such potentially destructive nervous energy, because a dog will respond to your relentless demands for immediate activity and amusing tricks far better than will most people, and he will certainly take more pleasure in doing so. Indeed, he lives for it.

A dog will provide you with an easy opportunity to practice your benevolence.

Many people find dogs much easier to engage in carefree, cheerful, and generously kind interaction than they do their other students, subordinates, or dependents. With enough practice enjoying benevolent experiences with your dog, you may develop the penchant for engaging in benevolent behaviors to such a degree that it bolsters your leadership effectiveness in all aspects of your life.

A dog will provide you with dogged devotion.

Most people, including most managers, desire some admiration and devotion from those they seek to lead. Such rewards from one's human followers can be difficult to earn on a continual basis, because most human subordinates expect so much more from you than will a dog. On the other hand, dogs seem very willing to provide this tribute without too many strings attached. I suspect that this is just a natural consequence of the relative ease with which most people treat their dogs benevolently.

Dogs are fun.

Fun is a good thing, and everyone needs more of it. Dogs provide a wonderful opportunity for sharing fun. Try to make having fun a focus in all of your relationships.

A Different Perspective on Ownership

While the pleasures of performing the owner's role well can provide much satisfaction, the most selfishly beneficial reason to excel as an owner is that you will then have a dog that is better behaved, more compatible, less hassle, and more fun. Good owners are good managers, and good managers develop good subordinates.

Given that you have read this far, I assume that you want to be a good owner. Being a good owner means that you are also a good caretaker, a good manager, and a good trainer for your dog. In any of these leadership roles, you will perform best if you make it a point to take the time to look at things from different perspectives.

In this chapter, we consider ownership from a dog's perspective as we examine what a dog can hope to enjoy through the care of a good owner. Not surprisingly, these sources of satisfaction have much in common with what anyone would value in a good boss.

A good owner takes care of my needs.

While I might be able to take care of many things on my own, my owner helps me get food, shelter, assistance with care for my health, and many other things. Without a good owner, my prospects for getting along in this world would be dire.

A good owner increases my usefulness.

While my owner teaches me to do the things he wants me to do, this also helps me become more useful and important to my owner and maybe even to others who can care for me. The more useful and important I am, the better those who need me are likely to treat me. I like being needed and important, because it helps me to get more of what I want.

A good owner stimulates me.

Face it: My life as a dog can be somewhat boring and purposeless. Just laying around all day, waiting for my next meal, isn't exactly living life to its fullest. When my owner engages me in things like going for walks or training or playing or other things he wants me to do with him, I feel more alive, adventurous, and full of purpose.

A good owner does not waste my time.

A good owner does not make me do stupid things for no reason. Because he is a good owner, the things he has me do have a good purpose, even if I don't always know exactly what that is. Often, they are just a good way for me to get what I want from my owner, and that is just fine with me.

A good owner gives me more control over what happens to me.

Not only does a good owner teach me what he wants; he also teaches me how to get what I want. When I want something, I know what I have to do to get it, and I know how to do it because my owner has taught me. I like having the control over what happens to me; my good owner teaches me how to have that control.

A good owner listens to me and lets me teach him things.

One of the best things about having a good owner is that when I try to tell him things, he tries to understand and do something about it. I am happy that my owner has learned to do most of what I ask of him and that he is trying to learn to do it faster and better.

A good owner is fun for me.

I like having more fun. Doesn't everyone?

Similarities and Differences

In these final closing remarks, I would like to celebrate a few enlightening if not amusing similarities shared by humans and dogs. Following that, in accordance with the promise that I made earlier in this book, I will also point out some profound differences that we must recognize and respect as we move back and forth between our leadership roles as dog owners and our managerial roles directing the activities of humans. The roles that we play, while similar in many ways, are also obviously quite different.

I hope that this review will reinforce much of what we have been studying about applying human management skills when training dogs and, as role-appropriate, about applying what we have learned about training dogs to the challenges of leading in our everyday lives.

Similarities

Both humans and dogs are intelligent creatures, driven to fulfill their basic needs.

Both are predators that historically have had to fend for themselves by initiating actions to satisfy their basic needs by cooperating and competing with others of their same species. Each employs an internalized set of rules that drive behavior to get what he wants.

Each is much more concerned for his own well-being than he is concerned for you. (Why wouldn't he be? Are you not more concerned for your well-being than you are for that of your boss?) Such self-directed interest has contributed to the survival of each species throughout the millennia.

Neither will offer you unconditional love. (This may sound like blasphemy, dog lovers, but it is true. However, you can always try to offer unconditional love to your pet.)

Each will submit to your leadership willingly if and only if he perceives sufficient value for doing so. (Empowerment to manage or train must be earned.)

Both species learn by observing of cause-and-effect associations.

In both species, the repeated consistent observation of an association increases the expectation of future observations of that association. One caution is that this characteristic makes both species highly susceptible to unintentional training. Regardless of the species, simpler associations are easiest to recognize and learn.

Both will seek and respond to good leadership.

Intelligent social creatures are most comfortable with some degree of predictable order and tend to seek leaders who give the impression that they can provide a means to achieve such order. Deference to appropriate leadership initiatives provided by others is important to maintaining effective relationships and social structures. Acceptance of leadership provides a path for members of either species to achieve much of what they want and need.

Intelligent social creatures dependent upon you will seek alternative sources of leadership if you do not provide it.

Both species respond best to clear directives.

Regardless of your subordinate's species or intelligence, the clearer you are about the direction you provide, the better he can understand and follow it. Complexity can obscure comprehension.

Both humans and dogs seek rewards through their interactions with others.

Both are highly social creatures that seek the support and acceptance of their peers and others. Both seek to influence the actions of others through their interactions. Both enjoy hearing their names in a positive context or friendly tone. Both enjoy lavish praise; the more sincere and warm, the better it feels. (While gratuitous praise may likely raise suspicions of your human subordinates about your motivations, have no fear of such a reaction from your dog.)

Both feel badly when being reprimanded, usually much more so than they show.

As a good leader, you must reprimand your followers' behavior when warranted. Whether it is with your human subordinate or your canine pet, the transgressor is usually already aware of and feels uncomfortable about the breakdown even before you begin your reprimand. Expect obedience when you reprimand, but do not expect remorse from either species. Pushing a reprimand too far will threaten the basic security of any follower. Always keep in mind that your follower's expectation that you will provide for his security is the main reason that he tolerates your leadership.

Both react more to difference than to sameness.

Maintaining the status quo is comfortable, because there is little compulsion felt to change or adapt to it. On the other hand, difference motivates reactions, adaptations, and new behaviors. The greater the difference, the more stimulating it is. In order to promote new and different behaviors, increase the contrast in the consequences you provide to the behaviors demonstrated by your follower.

Both like to socialize with others of their own kind.

Only people can satisfy some human needs, and only dogs can satisfy some canine needs. While perhaps more obvious with humans, arranging social activities for your pet to play with others of his species is an important role for you as his leader.

Both occasionally need to be cleaned up after.

Just like their leaders, sometimes your subordinate, student, dependent, or dog will make a mess. (On occasion, you may be the only one who even sees it as a mess, but that is an entirely different matter.) Whenever possible, encourage your student or subordinate to clean up his own messes, because your mess-cleaning activities are not something on which you want to nurture his dependency. However, when cleaning up his mess is beyond his ability, then you, as the leader, must see to it. This is another of those many caretaker duties that makes you useful and thereby empowered to lead.

Both will help you teach them if you listen well.

Both humans and canines want to learn, albeit for somewhat different reasons. Each cannot help but give you feedback about his interest, mastery, and comfort with the learning process if you will only observe for that feedback closely enough. Reacting purposefully to any follower's feedback will make you a better caretaker, manager, and trainer.

Differences

One never has the rights of ownership over another human.

While we may question whether anyone actually ever has full ownership prerogatives over a dog, I believe the level of dependency that humans have created for dogs in our environment mandates exercising many prerogatives of an owner, including those over life and death, in a humane, caring, and responsible manner.

Never attempt to exercise any prerogatives reserved solely for owners over another human. If you cannot entice the results you want through the options rightfully available to you as a manager or trainer, then you must either accept the situation or terminate the relationship as entitled by your role.

You are absolutely responsible for the well-being of your dog.

You created your dog's dependency on your care by bringing him into an environment for which he is not naturally equipped without human help. By taking possession of a dog, you assume all responsibilities associated with his health, cleaning, feeding, and happiness as well as a responsibility to any others that he might affect by his actions. Anything less is abuse of your dog or others in the society to which you have introduced him.

Except as a caregiver for a dependent who has become helpless without you, you are never responsible for another human in the same way that you are for your dog. You should expect that another human can and will pursue his own well-being independently in all matters beyond those for which you have rightfully assumed control. Acting otherwise with a human subordinate will promote a dependency that will almost certainly weaken him by compromising his self-sufficiency. This is not to say that helping another human is not good or proper; it is simply a caution to be aware of the differences between helping a subordinate as warranted and creating unwarranted dependencies in him.

It is really quite okay to have your dog do silly tricks solely for your amusement.

After all, you do own the dog, and it provides him an opportunity to please you. Just be sure when training him that your intensity is consistent with the fact that they are merely silly tricks and, when he performs them, that you let him know he has pleased you. Humans, on the other hand, deserve a bit more respect relative to the things a good leader would ask of them.

Your human subordinate may someday become your boss.

While it is highly unlikely that your dog will ever be in a position of authority over you, I have seen many situations in which individuals who were subordinate at one time went on to become a manager. Train your human students to lead in the way you would want to be led; it could end up benefiting you more directly than you might suspect.

Saying "please" is useless additional noise when giving your dog a directive.

Frequent use of the word "please" is expected of polite humans, particularly of polite managers and trainers, as an accompaniment to a command or a request. It properly acknowledges the status of your subordinate as a fellow human being. It indicates appropriate and deserved respect while further promoting acceptance and compliance with your leadership.

Omitting the word "please" shows rude disrespect in many human societies and may diminish the effectiveness of a directive. Similarly, proper and frequent use of the expression "Thank you" is also important with humans.

Unless specifically trained to do so, your dog does not expect, understand, or possibly even deserve the respectful acknowledgment that the word "please" imparts. Saying his name before giving the command opens the channel more effectively. Moreover, a dog is likely to be confused or delayed by such extraneous noise when trying to interpret your command. Extra verbiage is fine in the context of making social noises with your pet, but do not cloud your commands this way. On the other hand, saying "Thank you" or something like "Good dog" as a form of postperformance acknowledgment reinforces his showing of good behavior.

"Excuse me" is appropriate when causing a disturbance to either species. "Move it!" will work just about as well with your dog, but it may not come across as being quite as gentle because of the likely tone of delivery. Consider which you are intending to convey—a gentle alert or a barked command for instant movement—and keep in mind that your dog also learns how to treat others from how you treat him.

Tail wagging is always honest.

I have seen many dogs exert extraordinary efforts to cover up unapproved behaviors when caught in acts like purloining food or sleeping on forbidden furniture. However, I have never seen a dog that could hide the feelings displayed by the movements of his tail. Wouldn't it be wonderful if it were this easy to determine how people really feel about something?

A dog will stop barking as soon as his problem goes away.

If your dog barks unhappily, it means he perceives a problem, but as soon as you address the cause of his problem, he will typically stop. Unfortunately, you cannot count on such transparency in your human organization. I suppose it to be a social complexity thing.

It is good and proper to pet your dog lavishly all over his body whenever you feel the urge.

While doing so with human subordinates would fly in the face of every modern personnel best practice, you do own your dog, and once he learns to enjoy it, petting him lavishly provides a great opportunity to please him with no real potential downside for either of you. Enjoy it!

About the Author

Doug Morgan is a San Franciscan who came from Middle America in the mid-seventies to escape the perils of a life in academia. From a very young age, Doug has held a strong affection for dogs of all breeds and was fond of training tricks to his neighbors' dogs. His parents refused pleas to get a family dog until his early teen years, but when they finally did bow to the persistence of all six of their children, they embraced their first dog ownership experience big time by getting a beautiful Irish wolfhound puppy for the family with no idea how to train or care for her. She was loved, and she thrived nonetheless.

Since then, Doug has owned, lived with, and interacted with a great variety of dogs, most of them very good (or at least eventually so). He believes that proper training and socialization is the solemn duty of every dog owner and that virtually every behavioral problem a dog manifests stems back to the owner's mistakes in leadership.

Doug's formal education was in the physical sciences and abstract mathematics; his professional career includes twenty years as a senior executive in several major organizations in fields related to computer systems technology, technical staffing and project management, sales, and general business consulting. In 2001, he founded his own consulting firm, along with two associates.

After launching his practice, Doug focused primarily on serving business owners and managers who were seeking help to improve their organizations. Almost always, the problems he found most in need of correction were the results of ill-advised leadership actions. Upon recognizing that this was just like dog problems he had often encountered; given his penchant for drawing lessons from abstractions and his love of dogs, people, and good leadership, *Dog Training for Managers* was spawned and has now come to life.

Printed in the United States
By Bookmasters